D1283615

N        Lawson, Mark
6768        Conflicts of
L3    WITHDRAWN    hn Kean
1995        wson.
                39924000254033

Garland County Community College
Library
Hot Springs, Arkansas 71913-9174

GAYLORD

# JOHN KEANE

**Portrait of the Artist as a Small Boy** 1990
Oil on canvas
76.5 × 61 cm/30 × 24 in
Private Collection, UK

Conflicts of Interest

# JOHN KEANE

## MARK LAWSON

MAINSTREAM
PUBLISHING

EDINBURGH AND LONDON

in conjunction with

Angela Flowers Gallery

GCCC Library
101 College Drive
Hot Springs, AR 71913

*For Rosemary McGowan*

Copyright © Mark Lawson, 1995
All rights reserved
The moral right of the author has been asserted

First published in 1995 by
MAINSTREAM PUBLISHING COMPANY (EDINBURGH) LTD
7 Albany Street
Edinburgh EH1 3UG

ISBN 1 85158 752 7 (cased)
ISBN 1 85158 804 3 (paper)

No part of this book may be reproduced or transmitted in any form or by any means without written permission from the publisher, except by a reviewer who wishes to quote brief passages in connection with a review written for insertion in a newspaper, magazine or broadcast

A catalogue record for this book is available from the British Library

Designed by James Hutcheson

Typeset in Monotype Van Dijck and Helvetica Black by Litho Link Ltd, Welshpool, Powys, Wales

Printed and bound in Hong Kong by H&Y Printing Ltd

John Keane is represented by Angela Flowers Gallery
Flowers East
199–205 Richmond Road
London E8 3NJ
Tel. 0181 985 3333
Fax. 0181 985 0067

# Contents

# Conflicts of Interest

JOHN KEANE has the probably unique distinction for a British artist of having been the subject of an editorial in *The Sun*. The circumstances in which this occurred are described in Chapter Seven of this book, but the general observation can be made here that it was entirely fitting that Keane's work should end up making headlines as his work was made out of the headlines.

If a stranger looked at John Keane's passport – with its stamps for Nicaragua, Guatemala, Belfast and the Gulf during a three-year period – they would assume that he was either a journalist or a spy. If told that his work had also touched on the Falklands War, the British coal-mining industry and the impact on Britain of Thatcherism, they would conclude that he was definitely a television or newspaper reporter. More than any other modern British artist, Keane has demonstrated a desire to get out of the studio and into the social and political frontline. What he produces is a kind of editorial art.

It should perhaps be explained at this point that it was Keane's own idea that this assessment of his work should be written by someone who is a general and political journalist rather than an art critic. Like his decision to have the preface to one of his exhibition catalogues written by the comedian Alexei Sayle, it is a measure of a desire to place himself somewhere outside the traditional boundaries of the art world.

But, if one obvious reason why this book is called *Conflicts of Interest* is its subject's interest in conflicts – military, social and psychological – the title also touches on other important aspects of Keane's work.

His engaged style of work is clearly in conflict with other artistic traditions, from abstractionism to lyricism. His Nicaraguan or Guatemalan landscapes, for example, would probably irritate, for different reasons, admirers both of Warhol and Turner. Indeed, work like Keane's – broadly representational but highly politicised – sometimes seems like culture's joke against those right-wing critics who complained that they didn't like abstract art because they didn't know what it was about. Now here was art where they knew perfectly well what it was about, and that was exactly why they didn't like it.

And there is also another important conflict in Keane's art. The shadow of photography and television, usurping any claim by art to provide a mere record of experience, has been a problem for all late twentieth-century representational painters. Keane, however, not only invites the fight by working directly in the territory of the camera – wars, politics and other news stories – but frequently makes his paintings from photographs, either his own, taken on location, or those sampled from television and newspapers. His work is constantly in competition or uneasy co-operation with these rival visual forms.

As well as my own observation of the paintings, the monograph that follows makes use of five long interviews with Keane, recorded at his studio in east London between January and May 1995. For historical and political information, I have drawn on my own notebooks from the period, but also the following books: *Chronicle of the Twentieth Century* (Longman, 1987), *The Oxford Companion to Politics of the World* (Oxford, 1993), *The Battle for the Falklands* by Max Hastings and Simon Jenkins (Pan, 1983), *The Downing Street Years* by Margaret Thatcher (HarperCollins, 1993) and *The Columbia Encyclopaedia* (fifth edition, Columbia University Press, 1993).

That such a bibliography should be listed before a work on a painter is perhaps another illustration of the unusual nature of Keane's project. As what follows makes clear, Keane is exceptionally fond of puns in his titles, so perhaps the last observation of this introduction should be that this monograph is an attempt to explain how he came to find his place in *The Sun*.

Photograph © Nick Turpin/*The Independent*

**Sleeping Wolf** 1989
PVA on paper
114 × 84.5 cm/45 × 33 in

# The Morecambe and Keane Show
## *Early Years 1954–72*

THE HERTFORDSHIRE town of Harpenden, where John Granville Colpoys Keane was born on 12 September 1954, is not a famous location, but it did play a small part in the histories of British comedy and politics as well as making a contribution to the history of British art.

The comedian Eric Morecambe lived there until his death – the local public hall is now named after him – and, during his famous television shows with Ernie Wise, was given to yelling 'Harpenden!' as an expression of alarm when surprised during a sketch. Then, in 1979, the political constituency of St Albans, of which Harpenden forms a large part, returned a new Conservative MP in succession to Sir Victor Goodhew, the unambitious veteran backbencher who had just retired. Goodhew's replacement was Peter Lilley, a right-wing ideologue who rapidly became one of the standard-bearers of the Thatcherite revolution and remained one of those keeping the former prime minister's flame ablaze in the Major cabinets after her fall.

The St Albans part of the constituency, left to itself, might narrowly return a Liberal Democrat or Labour member, and it has been the influence of the solidly Conservative Harpenden and its surrounds which made it a safe seat for Lilley and his predecessors. A number of the more reactionary letters to the *Daily Mail* and phone calls to Radio 4's *Call Nick Ross* come from Harpenden. It is a Volvo-and-Labrador place, a commuter community serving London: a sort of five-star dormitory town.

The artist's father, Granville Keane, was a classic inhabitant. He commuted from a big old Victorian house in Wordsworth Road to London, where he worked as a stockbroker for Shepherd's (later Shepherd's & Chase, and now submerged within other firms). Granville had been born in the west of Ireland, but his family had moved to England (Southampton and then Bedford) when he was five, because, his son understood, of 'the fermenting Irish troubles. They had a landed gentry background, I believe.' During the Second World War, Granville spent three years in a Japanese prisoner-of-war camp.

Keane's mother, Elaine Violet Meredith Doubble, had a longer connection with Harpenden. Born in Scotland, she had grown up and been educated in the Hertfordshire town after her family moved there after the First World War. Granville Keane was her second husband. Her first had been killed in the Second World War. He was an Irishman and his County Down connections would subsequently be significant in the artistic career of John Keane.

The household in which John grew up in Harpenden comprised Elaine, Granville, two sisters and a half-brother from his mother's first marriage.

'Looking back,' he says, 'there was very little cultural input from my home life. They read books and listened to music but it was pretty lightweight stuff. There was negligible input on the visual arts. It was not a world with which they were in any way familiar . . .'

John was the youngest of the family and, in the fashion of the class, while his sisters were educated locally, he and his brother were sent away to board, first at Cheam prep school near Newbury in Hampshire, and then at Wellington, the blue-chip and military-orientated public school.

There is a long history of the English public-school system politicising its more artistically-minded charges in a left-wing direction. The playing-fields of Eton and elsewhere spawned first a generation of spies – Philby, Burgess, Maclean, Blunt – and then a generation of left-wing novelists and playwrights:

David Hare and Christopher Hampton (Lancing), and Salman Rushdie (Rugby). Given the oppositional and polemical quality central to Keane's art, it is clearly tempting to see him as a beneficiary of the same process, reacting against Harpenden and Wellington in his choice of stance and subjects.

'I don't think it was that there was anything about Harpenden, Wellington or that quintessential middle-class background that I detested,' says Keane. 'I have to admit that I was actually pretty happy at my schools, although I hated being sent away each term. It was just that my horizons were broadened and so it obviously raises questions about what you have previously just accepted . . . Also, because I was growing up in the '60s, and beginning to think for myself, I was quite aware of the changes in attitude that were going on.'

Although the social impact of early satirical vehicles such as the magazine *Private Eye* and the television series *That Was the Week That Was* is sometimes overstated, there is no doubt that the '60s did see a significant diminution in automatic social deference and respect for politicians. This was partly a product of Britain's military and political humiliation during the Suez Crisis of 1956, which was widely believed to be the nation's last imperial adventure, although as Keane's generation would later discover – and his work would reflect – this turned out not to be the case.

For Keane, the fact of the '60s in his background is more biographically relevant than either his birthplace or his education: 'There may have been an element of reaction against the public school, but the more important thing was that atmosphere of dissidence and counter-culture. Rebellion was in the air.'

Biographies of the creatively talented are always in search of the first significant recognition by outsiders – the kindergarten teacher who mutters, 'Oh, he does do a lovely drawing, Mrs Poussin' – but Keane can recall only that, from a young age, he liked to make pictures in exercise-books. It was at Wellington, between 1968 and 1972, that he became serious about art, and was encouraged by teachers to pursue what they seemed to recognise as a talent.

At the age of thirteen, Keane became a devoted surrealist, and worked for some time in the style of Magritte and Dalí. 'I think I did recognise it as a rejection of the order and conformity that was very much part of my background,' he admits. 'There was something I identified in there that subverted a large part of my upbringing.'

Wellington traditionally tunnelled its brighter sons into Oxbridge and its dumber ones into the army. There was no real precedent for what Keane began to suspect at the age of fifteen he wanted to do: move on to art school. A bet-hedging selection of A-levels – maths, physics, English, art history – may have reflected the hope of his parents and teachers that he might find an alternative ambition.

Keane remains grateful to Wellington for the art history course: 'I think it was rather well taught. It's still there in my head as a mental encyclopaedia that I refer to.' At the time, he was also using the theoretical lectures as a route map for his own experiments. 'After surrealism, I worked my way rather rapidly through most of the major art movements of the twentieth century. From Mondrian to Rothko, I glided through various techniques. By the last year, I was heavily into abstract paintings.'

His art teacher had sent away for prospectuses on various art courses and Keane chose Camberwell in London. His parents were eventually supportive, although they would have preferred a more reliable career. John Keane was offered, and accepted, a place on the foundation course at Camberwell, beginning in September 1972.

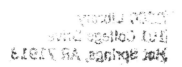

# From Camberwell to Moscow via Milton Keynes
## *Early Work* 1972–82

KEANE'S TIME at art school (1972 until 1976) coincided with one of the most volatile periods of post-war politics. In America, the Watergate burglary-and-corruption case led to Richard Nixon becoming the first president ever to resign under threat of impeachment. In Britain, minority Labour and Conservative administrations – led by Harold Wilson and Edward Heath respectively – alternated in office. A miners' strike in 1973 – and the determination of Prime Minister Heath to defeat union power and control wage-rise inflation – led to a period of power-cuts, the introduction of a three-day working week and an early television curfew to save electricity. A generation of schoolchildren learned to do their homework by candlelight. The year 1974 brought consecutive spring and autumn elections, before Wilson gained a small working majority in the second.

But, painting and drawing by candlelight, John Keane remained resolutely non-politicised. He remembers joining in with the majority of Camberwell students laughing at the ideologically committed artists, who were always attending meetings. One symptom of the student revolt at Camberwell led to the reorganisation of the school into commune-like studios under individual teachers, rather than the existing division into age-group years.

In general, though, he was more concerned with personal unrest than national chaos. 'Art school was a complete upheaval,' he recalls, 'after the background of public school. I can't really say that I enjoyed my time at art school. I was fairly disorientated and rather in a turmoil. And art school was quite a disappointment to me. I'd expected it to be a vibrant, intellectual place and it was rather small-minded and vindictive in a lot of cases. Most of the time, I was caught up in the growing pains of being nineteen and away from home and having all kinds of unhappy relationships with women.'

Artistically, after completing the foundation year, Keane ignored family pressure to sign up 'for something useful like graphic design' and opted instead for fine art, leaving for the future the question of how to make a living. The patron saint of the Camberwell teachers was Euan Uglow, who painted broadly from life but in an almost mathematical or geometrical way, involving detailed plotting of the intended image. Keane had little sympathy with this approach, and was drawn more towards photo-realism and Warholian manipulation of images, to which his teachers were unsympathetic: 'That was the pits for them, to work in any kind of very graphic way. The word "illustration" was the worst you could hurl at anyone who wanted to be a painter.'

In 1976, Keane graduated with a lower second, which left him feeling 'very peeved'. He went to work at the Inland Revenue Sorting Centre in Kew, where, even as a junior employee, he was required to sign the Official Secrets Act, though this willing submission to the apparatus of the state would apparently count for nothing when, fifteen years later, an artistic project would lead to his being vetted by the security services.

At this time, Keane had more or less abandoned any hope of full-time employment as an artist and contemplated a number of careers including – revealingly, as things turned out – journalism. But, in 1977, deciding to commit himself to painting, he advertised in the listings magazine *Time Out* for a studio and secured a room in the basement of a hairdressing salon in Chelsea. When this was reclaimed by the owner, he moved into the house in Cadogan Gardens of one of the salon's clients, laying plastic sheets

GCCC Library
101 College Drive
Hot Springs, AR 71913

**Interference** 1979
PVA on canvas
152.5 × 152.5 cm/60 × 60 in

**Rush Hour in Peking**
1980
PVA on canvas
183 × 152.5 cm/72 × 60 in

over the carpets before he started work. In the evenings, he was working as a waiter at Parsons restaurant in Fulham.

Keane's reticence about his talent as an artist is apparent from the type of work he was producing during this period, which attempted what might be called co-composition. He wrote off to several famous artists, asking them to send him a drawing or painting which he could subsequently incorporate in works of his own. Most – including Jasper Johns – refused (or, more likely, their galleries sniffily declined without asking them), but the Bulgarian-American artist Christo (Christo Vladimirov Javacheff), creator of the twenty-six-mile 'Running Fence' in California, despatched five signed postcards, which Keane used as collage material in prentice canvases of his own.

'I think that not very well-formed ideas about notions of authorship were behind all that,' he says. 'Also, I didn't have a very clear vision of what I wanted to do as an artist – and it probably reflected that as well.'

By the late '70s, Keane was established in a studio in Bury Street in Clerkenwell. His artistic heroes were Andy Warhol, David Hockney and Richard Hamilton. It is, though, the influence of Warhol that is most obvious in the use of pre-existing images, particularly of newspaper photographs. In one early work, Keane deliberately attempted to 'out-Warhol Warhol' through repainting by hand one of Warhol's silkscreen prints.

In 1978 Keane achieved his first exhibition, at a London club called the Zanzibar. He sold a couple of drawings – his first commercial success as an artist – but has subsequently suppressed this event from his published list of exhibitions.

In this period, he had given up being a waiter and found day-jobs which were broadly connected with art. From 1979 until 1982, he was employed by a shop called Miracles in the King's Road in Chelsea airbrushing duvet covers and cushions: 'Flamingos and palm trees and all that California stuff,' he recalls, 'for rock stars with no taste.' That job led to a commission to paint backgrounds for a film, *The Zany Adventures of Robin Hood*, a little-known comedy epic starring George Segal.

In 1980 there took place the exhibition which Keane's curriculum vitae, omitting the Zanzibar, acknowledges as the official beginning of his career: 'Peking, Moscow, Milton Keynes' at Minsky's Gallery in London. This was a collection of pictures of the three cities, based on (in the case of Milton Keynes) the artist's own photographs and (for Peking and Moscow) propaganda images. Although two of the cities Keane chose were among the most politically significant capitals of the twentieth century – and even Milton Keynes, planned as a utopian community by a Labour government, held some resonances – this work is an artistic rather than a political exercise. The commitment which would become such an important part of Keane's persona remained dormant.

There are, though, flashes in this early work of the style and subjects that would later emerge. Even without direct political engagement, Keane had begun to draw on images and personalities from the news.

In this period of Keane's output, though, the approach is always apolitically ironic. *Number of People Engaged in a Topical Activity*, a 1978 creation, shows James Callaghan, the British prime minister from 1976 to 1979, walking to a waiting government limousine, surrounded by suited aides and with a line of blue-helmeted London policemen behind him. This painting was based on a newspaper photograph. Keane has no record of the event depicted, but it seems likely, from the size of the police presence, that the original was taken in mid-1977 at the G7 (Group of Seven) economic summit of leading Western industrial nations, chaired by Callaghan in London.

From the same year, *Jean-Paul Sartre and Simone de Beauvoir Speedboating with Fidel Castro* is Keane's

**Jean-Paul Sartre and
Simone de Beauvoir
Speedboating with
Fidel Castro** 1978
PVA on canvas
152.5 × 152.5 cm/60 × 60 in
Private Collection, UK

**Monday Blues** 1979
PVA on canvas
152.5 × 183 cm/60 × 72 in

colonisation for paint of a newspaper photograph depicting exactly what it says: the two great French intellectuals participating in holiday watersports with the Cuban president.

Like his early invitation to other artists to send him pictures to be incorporated in his own paintings, Keane's appropriation of newspaper images can be seen as both post-modernism – ironic comment on an existing piece of work – and as an indication of his difficulty at this stage in generating a personal visual style.

Espionage and terrorism were two headline subjects of the period to which the artist seemed particularly drawn in the newspaper images he collected. He produced a series of works called *Spies*, based on the unmasking in 1979 of the art historian (another post-modernist irony here) Sir Anthony Blunt as the 'fourth man' in the Philby–Burgess–Maclean spy ring from the 1940s. Keane also worked on a number of images connected with the German Baader-Meinhof terrorist gang.

He also became interested in the late-1970s' phenomenon of middle-class guerrillas. A 1979 painting, *Interference*, is based on a newspaper photograph of the American heiress, Patti Hearst. Child of the great newspaper family – her grandfather, William Randolph Hearst, was the model for Welles's *Citizen Kane* – she was kidnapped by the Symbionese Liberation Army in 1974, converted to their cause and imprisoned for participation in a bank raid. This painting also reflects what would become one of Keane's growing concerns: media distortion. He stuck layers of masking tape across the canvas, then peeled them off to give the image a flickering instability like a poorly-transmitted television picture.

*Monday Blues*, completed in the same year, features another rich American rebel: Brenda Spencer, the American schoolgirl who, at the start of a new week, peppered her form-room with bullets, killing several classmates. Questioned by police about why she did it, she replied: 'I don't like Mondays.' That phrase was later used by Bob Geldof as the title of a song which became a number-one hit for his band, The Boomtown Rats. Keane's work – using the same distortion technique as *Interference* – has a background pattern of television-sets, suggesting the importance of modern media fame in disseminating, and perhaps even partly motivating, the girl's act. The Boomtown Rats' video for their song later also used a television-set motif, although there was no connection between the projects.

These are early works, for which Keane himself has little real affection, and show an artist still searching for a subject and a style. In this regard, his ship was about to come in.

**The Civil Servant Explains About the Crisis** 1982
PVA, crayon and photo transfer on paper
56 × 76 cm/22 × 30 in

**The Individual in Relation to the Masses** 1982–83
PVA on canvas
122 × 152.5 cm/48 × 60 in
Leicestershire Collection for Schools

# Scrap Metal with Iron Lady
## *Painting the Falklands War* 1982–84

ON 31 MARCH 1982, a contingent of Argentinian scrap-metal merchants landed on the uninhabited but British-dependent island of South Georgia in the South Atlantic and planted their national flag. Whether or not history repeats itself as farce, it certainly has a way of starting as farce – the shooting of a minor archduke leading to a four-year global conflagration, the resignation of an American president beginning with a bungled burglary – and this small-time prank by Buenos Aires rag-and-bone men was to lead to one of Britain's strangest episodes of the second half of the twentieth century.

Two days later, at dawn on 2 April, Argentina invaded South Georgia's populated (2,000 souls) south-eastern neighbours, the Falkland Islands. The British prime minister, Margaret Thatcher, three years in office, at once despatched a task-force of ships to recover the Falklands. This was to be the world's first naval war fought with missiles.

For British liberals of Keane's generation, this conflict was a profound shock. (And there would be another similar one, involving him even more deeply, within eight years.) It was not that they had not expected a war – the prospect had lost them many nights' sleep since adolescence, and kept the CND stall in brisk business at any college freshers' fair during the '70s – but that they had not expected to *live* through one. The next war involving Britain would be the Third (and Last) World War, prosecuted with nuclear weapons by the USA against the USSR, with London, courtesy of its NATO obligations, caught in the fall-out. No one would survive it but for a few poor roasted souls scavenging for a final meal in crisped cities overrun by massive radioactive rats.

Hence the capital qualities of the Falklands War, at least for those who were opposed to it, were anachronism and paradox. Against all expectation, in a world replete with the *matériel* for mutual nuclear obliteration, a small war could be fought, involving not the superpowers but Britain's defence of an old colonial possession. And it was waged not by the silent atomic missiles of modern nightmares, racing the earth's curve at the push of a button in a bunker, but by a fleet of ships which had sailed across the seas for six weeks before joining battle. It would be possible to exaggerate the quaintness of the episode – the ships were firing not gunpowder cannon but Exocets, the most lethal non-nuclear missiles then available – but the whole thing seemed, to a generation raised on *Doctor Strangelove*, a bizarrely old-fashioned form of combat.

This retrograde tendency extended, opponents felt, to the national psyche. Margaret Thatcher, whose Churchill impersonation had been rehearsed often already in the merely metaphorical battles of domestic politics, now had the proper context in which to pursue the historical comparison that possessed her. The Union Jacks and weeping grannies on the docks at Plymouth as the task-force sailed seemed to many a throwback to an earlier age of colonialism and jingoism. Politicians and newspapers began to speak in single words and exclamation marks. 'Rejoice!' said Mrs Thatcher, standing in 10 Downing Street, when the news of the recapture of South Georgia was announced. 'Gotcha!' said *The Sun*, when the Argentinian ship the *General Belgrano* was sunk with the loss of hundreds of men. 'Traitor!' said those who supported the war to those who didn't.

Keane was twenty-eight at this time and describes himself as 'interested in politics in an oblique way, though I had no involvement in politics'. The Falklands War, however, as well as driving its supporters further to the Right, had the effect of pushing its opponents further to the Left, and it served to politicise the artist. He was appalled by the jingoism apparent in both the public mood and the tabloid press (though which came first is hard to judge).

The works he produced in response to the Falklands marked, for the artist, 'a turning-point from the rather detached and ironic stance I'd had towards my subject matter and towards a more direct engagement. And, although I now feel equivocal about a lot of this work, I think that is what is important about it. It marked a change of attitude.'

The Falklands sketches and paintings, which would be exhibited at the Pentonville Gallery in London in 1984 under the title 'War Efforts', introduced two aspects of Keane's work which would become central from now on.

The first was the use of titles. The titles given by early painters were often simply generic or descriptive: *Christ Washes his Disciples' Feet* or *Christina of Denmark, Duchess of Milan* or *A Woman Bathing in a Stream*. But subsequently, Magritte experimented with false-label joke-titles and abstract artists made a deliberate statement about the lack of literalness (or, still worse, literary-ness) in their work by using names such as *Composition 4* or *Repetition 3*.

Keane's titles, by contrast, are wordy, editorial, polemical and, generally, punning. As we will see, some of the later canvases come with twenty-seven words of explication. Rather more in the manner of a novelist than a painter, his works usually begin with a phrase or title scribbled in a notebook. While some painters resent any suggestion that their works might be 'read' in a sub-verbal way – an artist once angrily remarked that writers always like Magritte, because his style is essentially literary – Keane intends his titles to be part of the experience of viewing a painting.

Keane's second important artistic decision that is apparent even from the Falklands canvases is his attitude to the rival visual media. From here on, his pictures jostle with both the suppliers of modern technology – television-sets, computer screens – and their products: newspaper photographs, images taken directly from the television screen. There are two aspects to this. One is a simple wish to observe and record modernity. There may also be something of a feeling of freedom from artistic history. Any novelist will tell you that writing a scene in which a character watches television or makes a telephone call brings with it a tangible liberation: you are writing a scene which Austen or Tolstoy could not. Keane acknowledges that the same instinct may apply to painting a still-life of a computer rather than a fruit-bowl. He also says that he enjoys the paradox of reproducing with a few brush-strokes an image of something of extreme technological complexity.

However, Keane's willingness to include photographs and television images within his compositions is a decision of a different order. Throughout the second half of the twentieth century, painters have worked in the shadow of photography and video. Every artist – and, in particular, war artists, as Keane would become – has become used to the question about why anyone would bother with a brush and easel these days when they could use a Pentax or a Camcorder. Indeed, one of the reasons for the move from representational to abstract art in recent decades was a reaction to the camera's usurption of art as a medium of mere record. Many artists chose simply to ignore the existence of photography (or to decline to enter the debate about which is better) but Keane takes it on directly. His works swallow and alter and comment on the images of the rival form, as if to show that there is nothing to fear.

These traits – tell-all titles and a gung-ho attitude to the visual opposition – would become much more apparent in the later work, but they are already evident in the Falklands pictures.

*The Civil Servant Explains About the Crisis* combines simple drawings of planes and ships from the task-force with an image from television: the face of the Ministry of Defence press spokesman, Ian McDonald, whose dictation-speed delivery of the latest news from the South Atlantic at daily press conferences became a celebrated feature of the war for those in Britain. Keane's painting plays with the contrast between high-tech weaponry and Second World War-style government propaganda.

*Still-Life* (*Insult to Injury*) combines a typical Keane title pun with a characteristic image. In showing a vase of roses and glass of whisky beside a television-set and typewriter, the picture belongs to the traditional genre of still-life, but there is also an angry suggestion that the journalist typing up his stories and headlines from the television pictures is still alive, while hundreds of those who fought are dead. The roses and whisky (the latter also carrying the familiar slur on the journalistic profession) point up another image that was to become frequent in Keane's work: the way in which modern television sanctions easy and often callous voyeurism of suffering. And, again as he would do many times in the future, Keane pastes real contemporary newspapers – including the notorious 'Gotcha!' – on to the canvas as a foundation for the painting, some of which collage material remains visible.

*Bunch of Roses*, in which a newspaper with reports from the war lies casually across the corner of a living-room table adorned with flowers, is a variation on the idea of comfortable middle-class distance from suffering, which would become a key Keane theme. *Blue-Striped Breakfast Set* similarly intrudes death into a still-life. A colour magazine spread of an army recruitment advertisement lies across a breakfast tray.

**Still-Life (Insult to Injury)** 1984
PVA, crayon and collage on paper
76 × 99 cm/30 × 39 in

**I Could Do That** 1983
PVA, wax crayon and pencil on paper
55 × 74 cm/21½ × 29 in
Private Collection, UK

**The Meek Inheriting the Earth** 1984
PVA on canvas
152.5 × 122 cm/60 × 48 in
Private Collection, USA

The artist was also irresistibly drawn – as was the satirical cartoonist Steve Bell of *The Guardian* at the same time – to the large penguin population of the islands. *Nuclear Penguin Family*, showing a small group of the sea-birds in the middle of the frozen wastes, suggests that potential world conflagration, of which some believed the Falklands adventure might be the start, was risked for the welfare of penguins.

The Falklands War ended on 14 June 1982, when the British recaptured Port Stanley and the Argentinians surrendered. Some 254 British and 750 Argentinian lives were lost during the six-week conflict, which was never officially declared a war by the British government. In Argentina, the ruling military junta collapsed, although its civilian successors did not formally accept the end of hostilities until 1989.

In Britain, the conflict had many consequences. Margaret Thatcher, domestically unpopular at the start of the war, emerged from it as an electorally-invincible heroine and won the second of her eventual three victories on a tide of flag-waving the following year.

The new one-year-old centrist political force, the Social Democratic Party, which had gathered middle-class support so rapidly that Ladbrokes were quoting low odds against its leader, Roy Jenkins, becoming the next prime minister, never recovered from the Conservative restoration which the Falklands War achieved. Moderation was suddenly tangibly less popular than it had been.

Other consequences were perhaps less obvious to those acclaiming Mrs Thatcher as a new Boudicca. The cost of the conflict (£700 million) and of maintaining the islands forever as a fortress against possible future invasion would have an unquantifiable impact on Britain's economic troubles in future years. And Margaret Thatcher's hugely unpopular decision to allow President Reagan to use British bases for American bombing reprisals against Libya in 1986 was simply a diplomatic *quid pro quo* for American support during the Falklands conflict.

But, in a speech in Cheltenham a month after the war's end, Margaret Thatcher had no doubts about the victory's significance: 'We have ceased to be a nation in retreat. We have instead a newfound confidence . . . We rejoice that Britain has rekindled that spirit which has fired her for generations past and which today has begun to burn as brightly as before. Britain found herself again in the South Atlantic and will not look back from the victory she has won.'

It is an uncomfortable irony of a modern war that it will tend to make media stars of many of those involved in it who survive it. The Falklands launched into orbit the careers of the journalists Max Hastings, Brian Hanrahan and Robert Fox. Even two of the seriously wounded – Simon Weston, hero of the TV series *Simon's War*, and Robert Lawrence, hero of the BBC drama *Tumbledown* – achieved celebrity.

Keane, too, was a minor beneficiary. The Imperial War Museum purchased two of the Falklands paintings and the artist also signed up with the Angela Flowers Gallery, as it then was, in Tottenham Mews. It would take another war to make John Keane famous, but the Falklands had given him a battle-plan for his artistic career.

**Man with Bomber** 1984
PVA on canvas
183 × 152.5 cm/72 × 60 in
Private Collection, UK

**Jumbo** 1984
PVA on canvas
183 × 152.5 cm/72 × 60 in

**Romantic Encounter**
1984
PVA on canvas
183 × 152.5 cm/72 × 60 in

**Country Life** 1985
Oil on canvas
183 × 152.5 cm/72 × 60 in
Private Collection, UK

**The Speculators and the
Ideologues** 1985
Oil on canvas
256.5 × 175 cm/101 × 69 in

**Who You Are and What You Do** 1986
Oil and mixed media on canvas
244 × 173 cm/96 × 68 in

26

**Fast Forward (Illusions of Progress)** 1986
Oil on canvas
183 × 152.5 cm/72 × 60 in

**Landscape** 1986
Oil and collage on canvas
152.5 × 122 cm/60 × 48 in
Private Collection, UK

**Futures** 1986
Oil on canvas
183 × 152.5 cm/72 × 60 in
Collection: Chase Manhattan Bank, NA

**Three Monkeys on the Edge of the Desert** 1986
Oil on canvas
182.5 × 157.5 cm/72 × 62 in

**The Exchange** 1986
Oil on canvas
211 × 167.5 cm/83 × 66 in
Private Collection, UK

**The Emperor's New
Pose** *or* **Doing for
d'Offay** *or* **The
Importance of Being
Important** *or*
**The Pot Calls the Kettle
Black** 1985–86
Oil and mixed media on canvas
244 × 183 cm/96 × 72 in
Private Collection, UK

**Old Lie Café** 1989
Oil and mixed media on canvas
246 × 300 cm/97 × 118 in
Collection: Glasgow Museums: Art Gallery and Museum, Kelvingrove

**Freedom and Publicity** 1988
Oil on canvas
122 × 152.5 cm/48 × 60 in
Private Collection, UK

**A Bigger Bang** 1987
Oil and mixed media on canvas
168 × 213 cm/66 × 84 in
Private Collection, UK

**English Gothic (The Deviant)
(Clause 28)** 1988
Oil and collage on canvas
229 × 168 cm/90 × 66 in
Private Collection, USA

**Chorus** 1988
PVA and wax crayon on paper
114 × 83 cm/45 × 32½ in
Private Collection, UK

**A Fuck You Limo on the Streets of London** 1988
Oil and collage on canvas
124.5 × 94 cm/49 × 37 in
Private Collection, France

**Raising the Standard of Righteousness on the Moral High Ground** 1988
Oil on canvas
126 × 95.5 cm/49½ × 37½ in
Private Collection, USA

**The Pariah** 1988
Oil on canvas .
112 × 91 cm/48 × 36 in
Private Collection, UK

**Controlling Interest (a Latterday Baron Enjoys the Freedom of the Press)** 1987
Oil and collage on canvas
183 × 152 cm/72 × 60 in
Collection: Harris Museum and Art Gallery, Preston

**Bystanders and Martyrs** 1988
Oil on canvas
213 × 168cm/84 × 66 in
Private Collection, USA

**New British Landscape
(Gathering Intelligence)
No. 3** 1987
PVA and collage on paper
114 × 83 cm/49 × 32 in
Private Collection, UK

**That's Entertainment** 1989
PVA, wax crayon and collage on paper
114 × 83 cm/45 × 32½ in
Private Collection, UK

**A Portrait of the Artist Pretending to Be a Cultural Guerrilla** 1987
Oil and mixed media on canvas
117 × 91 cm/46 × 36 in
Private Collection, UK

# Our Man in Managua
## *Nicaragua* 1987–88

AS THE Spanish Civil War attracted left-wing artists in the 1930s, so did Nicaragua in the 1980s. The novelist Salman Rushdie, at that time famous only for winning the Booker Prize with *Midnight's Children*, made the country the subject of his first (and last) travel book, *The Jaguar Smile*, published in 1987. The playwright Harold Pinter campaigned on behalf of the country's ruling revolutionary government, and entertained its leader, President Daniel Ortega, at his home.

After completing the Falklands pictures, Keane worked on a number of disparate projects. A holiday to Egypt produced *Jumbo* (1984), in which a 747 aeroplane lifts into the sky in the background, while the foreground shows a vast statue from the Valley of the Kings, the head broken off and lying in the sand. It is an image of ancient and modern feats of engineering and also, perhaps, of the potentially ruinous effects of tourism.

Other works from this period between major exhibitions – although there were two small shows at the Angela Flowers Gallery: 'Conspiracy Theories' (1985) and 'Work Ethics' (1986) – drew on the political and social changes happening in Britain during Margaret Thatcher's second term. *Who You Are and What You Do* is a sensual swirl of images of the kind of conspicuous financial consumption which was a feature of this period, particularly among young dealers in the City of London. Champagne is sloshed back at crisp white restaurant tables, while a smart red sports car is parked in the top right-hand corner of the frame. The title implies that these people's only definition of existence is their employment.

A similar red car is one of the proud possessions of the faceless, but still somehow smug, yuppie couple in *Country Life* (1985). The man is looking at his watch, and has removed his jacket but not his tie in what seems to be a subversion of the myth of the timelessness and restfulness of country life. For these two, the rural is simply another item to be scheduled.

The most directly political of these paintings – 1987's *Controlling Interest (A Latter-Day Baron Enjoys the Freedom of the Press)* – shows a faceless (but probably Australian) tycoon, reclining on a kind of sofa made from newsprint (this is collage, using actual pages), while chatting on the telephone with the Manhattan skyline visible behind him. The implication is quite clear: that freedom of the press has meant freedom for a few men to take control of it.

But, after his frustration at being reliant on second-hand media images from the Falklands and what he felt to be the success of the Egypt pictures, Keane was looking for a project based on observation of a foreign country. And so, in 1987, he too became drawn to the nation of Nicaragua.

On 19 July 1979, Nicaragua had been subjected to the most internationally significant socialist revolution since Cuba twenty years earlier. It would also prove equally unpalatable to the government of the United States. For the second and third quarters of the twentieth century, after a first quarter of American occupation, the country had been ruled by the dynastic dictatorship of the Somoza family. Aggressively pro-American, the Somozas industrialised and expanded Nicaragua, but widespread corruption, including the misappropriation of relief funds after a massive earthquake in the capital, Managua, in 1972, led to the creation of a poor underclass and the alienation of international support.

Violent repression of internal dissent by the ruthless President Anastasio Somoza Debayle led President Jimmy Carter to withdraw American support in 1977. Two years later, Somoza was overthrown

**An Agricultural Worker from the South Pauses Outside His House to Reflect on the Problems of Insider-Dealing in the Markets of the North**
1988
PVA and collage on papger
114 × 83 cm/45 × 32 in
Private Collection, UK

**A Gringo in the Bus Station** 1987
PVA, wax crayon and collage on paper
114 × 83 cm/45 × 32½ in
Collection: Unilever

by the Frente Sandinista de Liberación Nacional (FSLN). Known colloquially in the salons of the West as 'the Sandinistas', these revolutionaries took their name from Augusto Sandino, who had led guerrilla insurrection during the American occupation in the 1930s.

Left-wing enthusiasm in Britain for the Sandinista government of President Daniel Ortega was perhaps less for itself (Ortega presided over economic decline and was himself intolerant of opposition) than for the fact that it was the target of extraordinary organised opposition from America. President Reagan channelled millions of dollars to the Contra rebels within the country. Demonising the Soviet-supported Sandinistas as communists, President Reagan on one occasion told the American people during a television address that the Contras were 'the moral equivalent of our founding fathers'.

When the Democrat-dominated Congress outlawed further CIA or presidential interference in Nicaragua, the Reagan administration created the so-called 'Iran-Contra' operation, which sought to channel the profits from illegal arms sales in Iran towards the Nicaraguan rebels. This scandal, which centred on the Reagan aide, Colonel Oliver North, blighted the presidencies of Reagan and his successor, George Bush, and at times seemed likely to end them prematurely.

Keane was attracted to Nicaragua because it seemed to him 'a kind of focal point of world history – one of those proxy wars that was representative of the Cold War era, where US influence and Soviet influence were vying. And, after overthrowing a brutal régime, an attempt was being made to reconstruct the country along socialist lines, which was of interest to me. In the end, I felt it was a conflict I could get my mind around. I understood the issues, whereas Afghanistan or the Iran-Iraq War, or whatever, would have been much more difficult to comprehend.'

Keane approached the Nicaragua Solidarity Campaign in London, who arranged for him to spend six weeks in the country in the summer of 1987 as a guest of the Asociacion Sandinista de Trabajores de la Cultura (the Sandinista Association of Cultural Workers), the Nicaraguan equivalent of the Arts Council. As it turned out, Keane was left to himself after about ten days and, although given lodgings in the house of a local artist, was hampered both by this lack of organised access and by his inability to speak Spanish.

In Nicaragua, Keane began to develop the working practices which would vary little on future research trips, and which would become one of the controversies surrounding his work. In Nicaragua he did not operate the traditional sketchbook of the observing artist through the ages, but relied on a Leica, a shorthand notebook and a bag for found materials and substances. Only later, back in the London studio, did he begin to make paintings, using his photographs, journals and finds as inspiration.

The Nicaragua trip produced a number of canvases and other works on paper, which were exhibited at the Angela Flowers Gallery in March 1988, under the title 'Bee-Keeping in the War-Zone'.

*The Ruin of Managua Cathedral Sits Uneasily in the Plaza de la Revolucion on the Fault-Line. The Hotel Intercontinental and the Bank of America Look on* looks, or rather reads, with its twenty-seven-word title, like a deliberate goad to those artists and critics who believe that art should be careful in naming itself so as not to forget that it is a visual rather than a literary medium. Far from believing this, Keane was by now emphasising that his titles were an integral part of his canvases by scrawling the words in red crayon across the bottom of the pictures.

What the painting shows is precisely what it tells. Managua Cathedral, optimistically built on a fault-line and never rebuilt after the earthquake of 1972, stands skewed on the left-hand side of the canvas. The hotel (always an uneasy and paradoxical presence in a Third World landscape) and the Bank of America (a colonial symbol no longer occupied by its first colonial landlords) loom at the foot of the hills. A peasant woman and two children are isolated in the foreground. The centre and the bottom margin of

**Sandino Vive** 1987
PVA, wax crayon and collage on
paper
114 × 83 cm/45 × 32½ in
Private Collection, UK

**House in a Storm** 1987
Oil on canvas
82 × 67 cm/32 × 26 in
Private Collection, UK

the canvas reveal Nicaraguan currency and local newspapers.

The use of collage as a layer beneath the paint was to become one of Keane's favourite techniques and, following on from the titles, adds a second literary element to the artist's work, particularly when, as later, more recognisable English-language newspapers are used. This inevitably raises the question of to what extent the 'show-through' elements are deliberately exposed. Keane says: 'It's largely serendipity. Sometimes I look down and see something in the collage that might be relevant and pointed and so I paint around it. Other times, it's a matter of chance.'

The largest painting, *Magic, Realism, Politics, Economics, Theology, Architecture, Bananas, Plate Tectonics and Survival*, which incorporates images from all the other paintings, including the cathedral, bank and hotel, has a quite deliberate border of American and Nicaraguan bank-notes. Alternating 1,000-cordoba notes with one-dollar greenbacks, this border makes its own point about inflation, for the local 1,000 and the American 1 are both small currency notes.

The title work, *Bee-Keeping in the War-Zone*, resulted from one of the few logistical lucky breaks that fell to the artist during his often frustrating trip. In a cinema queue in Managua, he heard a woman speaking English, introduced himself and discovered that she was an adviser to the Nicaraguan Ministry of Agriculture on honey production. She invited him to accompany her on one of her visits to a farm in the country. Keane was struck by how this normal rural activity of bee-keeping was here underwritten by the presence of an armed guard against possible Contra attacks.

Painting in oil, Keane creates a lush and sensual depiction of foliage and the red-slate roofs and whitewashed walls of farm buildings, in which the only discordant note is that in front of the stout farmer's wife stand a soldier in battle-fatigues and a small boy, presumably the son of the farmer, handling his machine-gun for size.

This set of paintings also included another type of canvas that would become standard in the artist's projects: the self-mocking self-portrait. Here it is called *A Portrait of the Artist Pretending to Be a Cultural Guerrilla* and shows an ominous-looking Keane holding what looks like a dangerous weapon (but was, in fact, a wooden toy gun purchased in Managua). The picture, which also clearly glances back to the armed boy in *Bee-Keeping in the War-Zone*, displays a self-consciousness about political art and the idea of a painter going to war-zones.

But Keane's nervousness about the kind of work towards which he was moving was not shared by its viewers. This proved to be the artist's most successful exhibition to date, both critically (*The Times* included him in a feature on young cultural stars) and commercially: every painting was sold. Looking back, it is clear that it was in Nicaragua that Keane discovered the combination of type of subject, method of research and form of painting that would constitute his mature style.

Before and after the Nicaragua paintings, he had worked on a number of individual paintings that touched on the financial triumphalism that gripped Britain and America in the 1980s under the economic boom (and, as it turned out, bust) encouraged by the policies pursued by Margaret Thatcher and Ronald Reagan.

A 1987 work, *God's Gift (The Cynic Pours Another Coffee)*, showed a commodities dealer idly playing the world markets with a telephone cradled on his shoulder while attending to his elevenses.

*A Bigger Bang*, completed in 1988, makes an explicit connection between sex and money, as does its title, playing on the phrase 'Big Bang' used in the City of London to describe the liberalisation and computerisation of trading on the Stock Exchange. (Economically, 'Big Bang' had indeed been followed by a bigger bang, when, on Monday, 19 October, 10 per cent was knocked off the price of shares in the worst single day's trading in history.) In Keane's painting, a couple are sexually entwined beside the smart trappings of financial dealership: computer, desk, telephone, commodities figures.

With its twenty-four-word title putting it close to the record held by *The Ruin of Managua Cathedral etc*, a 1988 canvas called *An Agricultural Worker from the South Pauses Outside His House to Reflect on the Problems of Insider-Dealing in the Markets of the North* directly reflects Keane's experience of returning from the poverty of Nicaragua to the rampant capitalism of the free-market West.

But, as he worked on these pictures, Keane was looking for another part of the world to research and paint. He chose one in which the designations 'North' and 'South' held a quite different meaning.

**The Ruin of Managua Cathedral Sits Uneasily in the Plaza de la Revolucion on the Fault-Line. The Hotel Intercontinental and the Bank of America Look on** 1987
PVA, wax crayon and collage on canvas
114 × 83 cm/45 × 32½ in
Private Collection, UK

**Ghost Town (The Spirit of Sandino Stalks the Ruins of Managua)** 1987
PVA, wax crayon and collage on paper
114 × 83 cm/45 × 32½ in
Private Collection, UK

**Bee-Keeping in the War-Zone** 1987
Oil on canvas
195.5 × 170 cm/77 × 67 in
Collection: The Arts and Museum Section of Cleveland County Library and Leisure Department, Gift of CAS

**Magic, Realism, Politics, Economics and Bananas** 1987
PVA and mixed media on paper
114 × 83 cm/45 × 32½ in
Private Collection, UK

**March of History** 1990
Oil on canvas
175 × 226 cm/69 × 89 in
Private Collection, UK

# Paintings on a Wall
*Northern Ireland* 1989–90

A RECURRING THEME in Keane's work since the Falklands paintings had been compartmentalised existence: the ease with which people can ignore realities they find disturbing.

The response of some people to this accusation is that they have to ignore some reality: the modern mass information media provide too much of it, and, anyway, many of these troubles are far away and no concern of ours. The difficulty with this defence is that one of the modern stories most ignored in Britain is not very far away at all, and is, historically and constitutionally, very much a concern of ours. It was to this subject that Keane now turned.

Since 1969, a bloody civil war was being fought within the United Kingdom, a few hundred miles from London, but the majority of the British people either ignored, or were bored by, this fact. When British soldiers were sent into Northern Ireland to keep the peace between (or keep apart) the Protestant and Catholic communities, it was briefly fashionable to describe the military intervention as 'Britain's Vietnam'.

But Vietnam convulsed a nation. In Britain, research soon showed, audiences for television documentaries and plays fell when they turned to the subject of Northern Ireland. The nearly-daily sectarian killings in Belfast soon became bottom-of-the-page fillers in the British press. Only when the IRA (Irish Republican Army) exploded a bomb in a British city did the coverage increase.

Searching for another country to be his subject, Keane thought, in 1990: 'It was all very well travelling around the world, but there was stuff that merited attention on my own doorstep. It had been going on, then, for twenty years, and, like most people, I had pretty much been content to ignore it.'

For Keane, the war footing of Northern Ireland since 1969 was even more perplexing than for most of the British, as his main association with the place was as a holiday destination. Until the 'Troubles' began, when he was fourteen, the artist would regularly spend family holidays in the seaside town of Newcastle, County Down. The Keanes retained links with the Northern Irish relatives of his mother's late first husband.

The concept of 'objectivity' is not one which has found much favour in the history of Northern Ireland. All outsiders, the rival sides believed, were prejudiced one way or another. There is an old Belfast joke in which a man asked his religion by a paramilitary replies, thinking himself canny, that he is Jewish. 'Ah,' comes the reply. 'A Catholic Jew or a Protestant Jew?' But Keane, who has no religious affiliation in adulthood, believes that he was as nearly objective as it was possible to be. 'I had no fixed sympathies,' he says. 'I was baffled and wanted to get underneath it.'

Keane spent a month in Northern Ireland in the summer of 1989, staying with relatives. A friend of the artist, employed by Ulster TV, arranged contacts with representatives across the community, including IRA sympathisers, its political wing Sinn Fein and the UDA (Ulster Defence Association), the Protestant terrorist force which, through the 1980s, seemed, to observers who thought themselves objective, to be coming to match the IRA in savagery and fanaticism.

As in Nicaragua, Keane used the journalist's tools of electronic Olympus and notebook. The title of the eventual exhibition, 'The Other Cheek?' – shown at Flowers East in March 1990 – emerged from this aural and visual sketchbook. Representatives of the UDA and Sinn Fein (in interviews with Keane) and

**Brick Wall** 1989
PVA, wax crayon and collage on paper
114 × 83 cm/45 × 32½ in
Private Collection, UK

a British soldier (in a TV documentary he saw) all used an identical phrase: 'What do you expect us to do, turn the other cheek?' This was particularly resonant in the context of Northern Ireland, where the Bible, one of the few things the warring sects shared, indeed instructed them to turn the other cheek.

Of the twenty-five works which comprise 'The Other Cheek?', only two small oils are not concerned with the Troubles. *Portrait of the Artist as a Small Boy* is a picture as happy as a holiday snap, which effectively it is, picturing the young Keane running excitedly towards the beach from the large colonial hotel during one of his Newcastle trips in the 1950s. Along with *Mournes* – a tranquil Irish landscape of sheep and drystone walls and hills – it is a deliberate reminder of the beauty of Northern Ireland in its prelapsarian state; or, given the long and tangled history of the province, an interlapsarian state in the middle of this century. The pun-sensitive artist may also have enjoyed the foreboding ring of the place-name: Mournes.

The rest of the pictures concentrate on the more expected images of Northern Ireland. Two linked paintings, both bearing the title *Brick Wall*, are quintessential Keane, working on the four separate levels present in the best of the post-Nicaragua work.

The first level is reportage, documentary evidence from the artist's field-work: these abusive murals, tit-for-tat images, were a reality of the Belfast landscape, and perhaps the sight that made the most vivid impression on most first-time visitors. The rival Catholic and Unionist wall paintings may, indeed, constitute the only literal example of war art.

The second level is what we might call the Keane sense of irony: a strain of artistic self-awareness or post-modernism. Keane, in these pictures, is painting a painting: a rare and intriguing technical exercise. And, of course, when hung, his painting of a wall painting will hang on a wall.

The third level is titular polemic or commentary. *Brick Wall* is another of the artist's jagged puns, invoking the idea a common-enough sentiment in England before the hopeful peace process of the mid-1990s – that debate with either side involved in the Irish conflict was as fruitful as talking to a brick wall; a charge which the communities seemed spectacularly to accept by, in Belfast, talking to each other with brick walls.

The fourth level is stylistic. Both *Brick Wall* compositions employ the favourite Keane technique of painting onto a collage of material from other media. Here, as with the Nicaragua pieces, newspapers collected during his visit have been pasted onto the canvas as an extra layer. As well as allowing the artist the option of leaving visible a significant or serendipitous stretch of newsprint, this technique may also be a kind of structural pun. Keane's paintings are, in two ways, based on newspapers. They are, literally, a gloss on the headlines.

The use that Keane makes of his research varies. Sometimes a picture builds on a single, witnessed image, to which Keane's thick and smeared oils lend a menace and grotesquerie which a photograph could not have communicated without an accompanying article.

*Flirting with History*, for example, recreates the scene at one of the traditional Unionist street parties the night before 12 July. Keane was struck by the way in which such ostensibly festive events were 'a celebration, but a provocation too'. His painting plays with this strange combination of the festive and the threatening.

In the foreground, young women giggle and young men drink as on a night-out anywhere. But flames swirl at the back of the picture. It is probably a bonfire, but Belfast is a city in which flames have been a regular sight and the viewer is suddenly aware of the irony of lighting a fire for pleasure in the city where it is so often lit for pain. Similarly, the street lamps hold an echo of searchlights.

Another curious detail is a large chalk outline of a hand on the ground. This may look like a surrealist interpolation by the artist, but is, in fact, witnessed reality. The 'hand of Ulster' is a Unionist motif, based on a legend that, when it was decided that the virgin land would belong to the one among its earliest settlers who touched it first on landing from the sea, a voyager cut off his hand and threw it on to the earth. Although relatively few viewers of the painting will be aware of this piece of Irish history, the image makes a contribution to the chilling atmosphere of the painting even for the ignorant. The chalked hand holds an unmistakable echo of the outlines drawn on the ground at murder scenes by the police.

In the same way, *March of History* is based on what Keane witnessed at one of the following day's marches. There are journalistic details, such as the dark glasses worn by the marchers, the legend 'No Surrender' on a drum, the acrobatics of the cheerleader. Keane, though, has lowered the perspective to make the marchers huge and looming. Their faces are distorted and unclear. The sky is thunderous. A victory parade has become a permanent declaration of war.

Keane seems to have interpreted 'objectivity' as being equally savage to both sides. Although a painting of an Orange Lodge rally – the faces again rendered sinister by distortion – is titled *Intransigence*, which has the ring of left-wing agitprop, the depiction of the Republican community employs the same tone and techniques.

**Flirting with History** 1989
Oil on canvas
173 × 241 cm/68 × 99 in
Private Collection, USA

**Murphy's Law, Enniskillen** 1989
Oil and collage on canvas
223.5 × 173 cm/88 × 68 in
Private Collection, UK

*Murphy's Law, Enniskillen* focuses on one of the IRA's most savage acts: the bombing of a Remembrance Day parade in 1987. This was to become a turning point in the Troubles. One of the few atrocities within the province in the latter stages of the conflict to produce headlines west and east of Belfast, it also reduced sympathy for the IRA both inside and outside Ireland and may have been a factor in the IRA's subsequent greater willingness to consider a negotiated solution. Gordon Wilson, the father of one of the victims, attracted worldwide credit after publicly forgiving his daughter's murderers, and subsequently became a key symbol in the peace process which would eventually lead to the IRA ceasefire and London–Dublin peace process of 1994 and 1995.

**Censorship, Human Rights, Murphy's Law and Kneecapping** 1989
Oil and collage on canvas
155 × 109 cm/61 × 43 in

**Peace-Giant** 1989
Oil and mixed media on canvas
228.5 × 157.5 cm/90 × 62 in

Keane's *Murphy's Law, Enniskillen* is based on a conversation he had with a Sinn Fein activist, who attributed the IRA 'mistake' on that bloody Sunday to 'Murphy's Law', the modern aphorism (also known as 'Sod's Law') which dictates that: 'If anything can go wrong, it will. At the very worst possible moment.'

On his research trip to the town, Keane browsed around a tourist tat shop, where he saw an Irish linen tea-towel for sale, printed with the text of Murphy's Law. Little signs from God like that keep writers and artists going, and, in Keane's completed canvas, the souvenir tea-towel lies at the base of the painting, alongside two British newspapers from the morning after the bombing, one of them visibly quoting Gordon Wilson's words about his daughter: 'My Angel's Gone To Heaven.' The rest of the painting plays on two savage ironies: of a war memorial coming to resemble a war site and a massacre occurring in a place where wreaths were already laid. Death, in Ulster, is piled on death. There is also an echo in the title of judicial expressions such as 'Martial Law' or 'Mob Rule'. Northern Ireland, the picture indicates, is under Murphy's Law.

Another of the paintings, *Watching the Sinn Fein Video about RUC Interference in Republican Funerals for the Seventeenth Time*, is based on a scene witnessed by Keane during one of his research trips. A teenage Sinn Fein sympathiser accompanied the artist on a tour of the Catholic parts of Belfast. They stopped at the house of one of the boy's mates, where tea was served.

Keane's picture captures an innocuous domestic scene – of family chat over char and biscuits – which is undercut by two troubling details. The two youths are wearing football shirts in the colours of the Scottish football team Celtic, a decision which speaks of far more than sporting allegiance and youthful fashion. For a young Irish Republican to support Celtic goes well beyond enthusiasm for soccer, as Scottish football has traditionally been divided on religious grounds, with Celtic staffed and supported by Catholics and their arch-rivals, Rangers, by Protestants.

This sense that even leisure is politicised is reinforced by the family's choice of television viewing, which, as the title explains, is a propaganda cassette about army harassment of Catholics. A recurring theme in Keane's work is the ease with which television's flow of information about the world can be ignored by the comfortable middle classes. Here, though, is the opposite extreme. These are people who do not want escapist entertainment but confirmative entertainment. The image also subverts a reassuring cliché of those who live in other parts of Britain. It was possible, they would often say, to 'sit in your front room in Belfast and not even know there is a war going on. Normal life continues.' But, as Keane's painting shows, those families at the head of the sects wanted to be reminded, even in their living-rooms, that there *was* a war going on. This, to them, was normal life.

The third group involved in Belfast – the British Army – features in several of the smaller PVA paintings on paper and dominates two of the larger oils. *Peace-Giant* is another Northern Irish landscape, painted, like *Mournes*, with an almost cod-Constable lyricism. This canvas, though, bears one important difference. The *Peace-Giant* of the characteristically ironic title is one of the army observation posts on the border near Armagh. Like an Easter Island statue – Keane has added a hint of eyes and nose to the square watching-box at the top – shored up by scaffolding, it looms over the cattle and sheep. It is as if a third, ancient and pagan, god watches over the two sides and their incompatible gods.

In the title painting of the collection, *The Other Cheek?*, all the sides in the conflict are depicted together for the only time, although they are deliberately fixed in their separate patches of the canvas, unacknowledging and unknowing of each other, like a moment in a stage play when parallel action from different locations, nations or even centuries is differentiated only by lighting.

On the left of the picture, beneath a mural of Republican paramilitaries firing skywards, a howling mother holds her dead child. On the right, under a mural of King Billy on his horse, a bald man in a shabby raincoat looks down at a corpse in a blue dress whom we assume to be his daughter, while an Orange Day parade disappears from the edge of the painting. In the centre foreground, a British soldier in combat fatigues is crouched over the bleeding body of a colleague. Further on, a burned-out car (broken-down automobiles being a recurring Keane motif) bulks against fencing, the casualty of either a car bomb or joy-riding. On the hills beyond, a line of corrugated fencing speaks of the realities of Belfast, while the Constable hills and sky beyond tell of what it once was. Each of the figures stares fixedly ahead, no cheeks are turned.

Crucially, the various tableaux are given equal weight. The artist has taken no sides, but, like most journalistic visitors to the conflict, has been struck by the apparent insolubility of the conflict. The paintings, though, are not negated by the slightly more hopeful prognosis which, as it happened, was to arise only five years later. Even if lasting peace were to occur, Keane's work in 'The Other Cheek?' would stand as a vivid historical record of the scenes and feel of Britain's forgotten post-war war.

**The Other Cheek?** 1989
Oil and mixed media on canvas
244 × 274 cm/96 × 108 in

# Going Underground
*Ollerton Colliery* 1990–91

LOOKING AT the curve of Keane's concerns between 1982 and 1994 – from the Falklands War via Northern Ireland to the Gulf War and recession-hit London – there is one striking absence in an otherwise full hand of Britain's political crisis points: the Miners' Strike of 1984. A little of the period's sense of social division and demonstration of state and police power seeps into the 'Conspiracy Theories' work of the mid-'80s, but, otherwise, the subject is unmined.

'It's a fair point,' says Keane. 'I might have been expected to deal with it. It seems a natural subject. But, for whatever reason, I didn't feel particularly involved in it at the time.'

In 1990, however, there was an opportunity for the artist to make good his omission. Nottinghamshire County Council invited him to produce the first exhibition for Nottingham's new Angel Row Gallery. The subject was to be the county's Ollerton Colliery, where Keane was invited to spend some weeks.

This was the first large-scale commission he had received and was a measure of the reputation the then thirty-six-year-old artist was gaining as a polemical realist. The council's artistic advisers had well understood that here was the perfect subject for Keane.

He was, though, initially reluctant: 'At that time, I wasn't even taking the London Underground, because I'd become slightly claustrophobic. But I went up – or, rather, down – for a day's reconnaissance and I thought, yes, okay . . .'

Keane's three weeks of photography, note-taking and interviewing at the colliery was subsequently turned into nineteen oil paintings, preserving in oil an industry destroyed by oil.

Although the Miners' Strike was six years in the past when Keane visited the colliery, neither the paintings, nor the average British viewer of them, can shake off associations with that period.

Ollerton was a pivotal pit in the strike, kept open by the Union of Democratic Miners (UDM), the new moderate opposition to the traditionally militant National Union of Miners (NUM), and thus the scene of much of the bitterest picketing and most high-profile policing. By 1990, many of the promises made to non-striking miners by the government and the National Coal Board about the industry's future were beginning to seem empty. And, in the month that Keane was present, the *Daily Mirror* published (subsequently discredited) reports about the financial conduct of the NUM president, Arthur Scargill, during the strike. Hence the mine was full of echoes, and so are the paintings.

The Ollerton work – collected as 'Cloth Caps and Hang-Gliding', which opened Nottingham's Angel Row Gallery in April 1991 – represented a considerable technical departure for Keane. For the first time in his mature work, there is almost no use of collage and different media. Although newspapers feature prominently in two of the works, they have a purely realistic function: they are what the miners were reading in the recreation scenes that Keane observed. And, except in some of the titles, where the artist continues to mine his rich seam of wordplay, there is no irony or post-modernist trickery. For the first time, Keane concentrates on portraits and some of his oils of individual miners could almost have been painted by a social-realist like Wright of Derby.

'The Ollerton work is deliberately much more direct than what has gone before,' Keane agrees. 'They're much more to do with observation and recording in a more literal way. I felt that the subject demanded it. It's not a modern, ironic thing these men are doing.'

**Fossil Fuel (1)** 1990
PVA and wax crayon on paper
112 × 84 cm/44 × 33 in
Collection: Hill Samuel Investment Services Group

**Face** 1990
Oil on canvas
244 × 305 cm/96 × 120 in

**Canteen** 1990
Oil and collage on canvas
127 × 96.5 cm/50 × 38 in

*Face* is typical of Keane's response to the Nottingham commission. The only wholly characteristic aspect of the work is the double meaning of the title. Miners work at a 'face' of coal, but the canvas is also dominated by the visage of an individual miner. The artist, too, is working at the face.

The miner in the foreground of *Face* is presented heroically. His eyes are bright and kindly, shining through the false tan of coal dust. He looks more proud than phlegmatic or oppressed. The tone or stance of Keane's painting seems to be simple admiration rather than pity or political anger.

Another portrait of a single worker, *Jim Turner*, is also in this heroic mode, Keane even going so far as to use a virtually unique example in his output of a literal, descriptive title. The painting is more impressionistic than *Face* – the miner's helmet smears and swirls of cream, his jacket sweeps of orange – but the same pride and kindliness radiate from his features.

*Canteen*, probably the most successful of the portraits, lies midway between Keane's signature style and the classicism of *Face* and *Jim Turner*. Two miners, filthy from the pit, are eating a meal in the colliery canteen. There is one collage element – a *Daily Mirror* headlined, in reference to the NUM scandal, 'Scargill: Fraud Squad cops go in' – but its presence is documentary. This is the paper one of the miners is reading with his tea. The thick tea, heavily-spread margarine and plate of pie and chips the other miner is eating are unusually suited to Keane's way with paint: laying it on dark and deep. The physicality of the artist's use of oils has here met a perfect subject in the murk and earthiness of the miners' world. There is also – for those who come to the painting from the artistic rather than the mining community – a painterly allusion. The composition nods to a Picasso work, *The Frugal Repast*, in which a man and woman are eating a meal.

Eight of the 'Cloth Caps and Hang-Gliding' canvases feature work or training methods and it is in these canvases that Keane brings out the danger of the miners' life. *Roof Bolting*, in which a miner is securing a tunnel support, carries with it the implication of potential roof collapse, the terror of every mining community. Even in the summer daylight, the miners are practising for the disasters that might visit them in the dark. Two small paintings feature *Fire Training*; another, *Competition*, is a study of life-saving practice; and a fourth, *Bunker Rescue Practice*, involves training in winching an injured or trapped colleague to safety.

This concentration on disaster drill, with all that it implies, is the artist's neat solution to the difficulty of how to be true to what he saw – and, thankfully, there was no catastrophe at Ollerton while he was there – and yet reflect the terrible reality that not only the livelihood of miners but their actual lives are at daily risk in their profession.

The threat to mining as an industry is hinted at in two of the pictures. *Fossil Fuel* takes a cross section of a modern industrial scene. Electricity pylons and a power station loom at the top of the canvas, while, at the bottom, below ground, a single bare-backed miner works at a seam. The miner is connected with the modern world above – indeed, it is he who provides it with power – but the link looks archaic and ridiculous. He looks like a relic; or, as the title suggests, a fossil. It is hard to believe that the chain of production can be sustained in a modern world.

*Double-Glazing* – a simple picture of a house in the Ollerton district – is another oblique reflection of the impact of modernity on the mining industry. The red-brick semi-detached in the pit village has double-glazing now. There are two purposes to double-glazing: one is to keep out the babel of the modern technological society – cars and aeroplanes – and the other is to keep in the heat from radiators which, being at the extremities of rooms, are most likely to lose it. It seems reasonable to guess that the home in the painting has central-heating rather than a coal fire. The car outside the house, the television aerials on the roof, the hint of a satellite dish on the wall are further hints of the gentrification and technical developments which threaten the future of the coal industry.

But the artist is also particularly alert in these works to the methods of his own industry. Artistically, Keane is exploring in these pictures the question of light source. This calculation, a necessity in all representational art, becomes particularly significant when painting a coal-mine, with its routinely crepescular conditions. There is also the irony that the point of coal-mining is to produce light, through electricity. Keane points out this connection by naming two of the more abstract canvases *Light Source*, in which, at the end of a tenebrous tunnel, there is a bulb-like burst of yellowish light. In *Face*, these men who are making light in the dark are guided by an old-fashioned miner's lamp or a battery-powered beam from their helmets. *Roof Bolting* puns visually on the idea of 'beams': plank-like lengths of illumination stream from the helmet lamps of the miners, paralleling the lengths of steel in the roof of the pit.

As with the Northern Ireland paintings, Keane's Ollerton portfolio aims to visualise a part of their history which British people are prone to ignore or forget. In their experiment with portraiture, they are a significant moment in the development of Keane's technique but they also, without ever explicitly touching on politics, fill in a missing chapter in the story which the artist's work was beginning to tell of Britain's economic and political journey since the beginning of the 1980s.

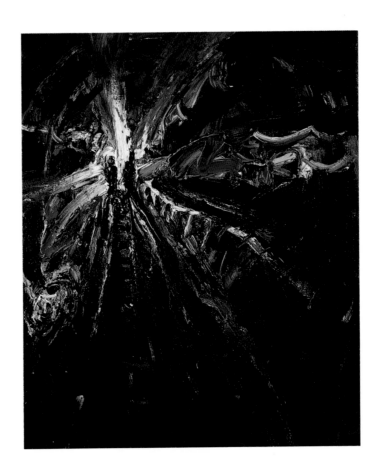

**Light Source (2)** 1990
Oil on canvas
61 × 56 cm/26 × 22 in
Private Collection, USA

**From the Rapid Loader**
1990
PVA and wax crayon on paper
112 × 84 cm/44 × 33 in

**Pint of Lager/Let's Do the
Timewarp Again** 1990
Oil on canvas
109 × 84 cm/43 × 33 in
Private Collection, USA

**Ecstasy of Fumbling
(Portrait of the Artist in a Gas Alert)** 1991
Oil and mixed media on canvas
152.5 × 107 cm/60 × 42 in

**John Keane in the Saudi Arabian desert**

# A Place in the Sun
## *Painting the Gulf War* 1991–92

SADDAM HUSSEIN, who took over the presidency of Iraq's ruling military government in 1979, had a definite, if somewhat specialised, interest in modern painting. He collected massive portraits of himself in the heroic mode, which were on display on walls and hoardings and in public buildings in his country's capital, Baghdad.

The events which were to make Saddam Hussein the latest subject of a modern English artist began on 2 August 1990. Iraqi tanks and aircraft moved across the border into Kuwait, its tiny but, because of oil, infinitely richer neighbour. The television and radio stations and government buildings were seized. The nation's ruler, Emir Sheikh Jaber Al-Ahmed, fled to Saudi Arabia.

The fact that the Soviet Union voted alongside America to condemn the invasion that night at the United Nations was evidence of the much-vaunted 'new world order' which, according to America's president, George Bush, would follow the collapse of communism. However, the fact that the invasion had happened in the first place was evidence that the Cold War would simply be followed by international tension elsewhere: in, for example, the Middle East. The second war involving Britain during John Keane's adult life was beginning.

The last four months of 1990 saw a stand-off between Saddam Hussein and the international community. Tedium was interspersed with tension as President Mubarak of Egypt and King Hussein of Jordan tried to broker various Arab solutions and the United Nations passed resolutions and issued ultimatums, most of which originated with George Bush. Finally, in United Nations Security Resolution 678, passed on 29 November, Saddam Hussein was given a deadline of 15 January 1991 to leave Kuwait. If he did not comply, military force would be employed.

These twenty or so weeks from the end of one summer to the beginning of the next winter were a kind of 'phoney war', equivalent to the period between the declaration of the Second World War and the outbreak of hostilities. From the very start of the crisis, there was a huge Western military presence in the Middle East. American troops had rushed to Saudi Arabia, at the invitation of its ruling royal family, as soon as Kuwait was invaded. It was feared that Saddam Hussein might carry on from Kuwait City towards Riyadh. The politicians spoke of defending freedom, but this was complicated, for Kuwait was not a democracy, and it was widely believed that the West was defending oil prices, not necessarily a reckless motive in an industrialised economy, but a practical crusade rather than a moral one. In Washington, the anti-war protestors chanted: 'Hell, no, we won't go! We won't die for Texaco!'

With this threat averted by the US military presence, President Bush began to construct 'Operation Desert Shield', a multinational defence force to confine the Iraqi army to Kuwait and then put pressure on them to leave. Although the initial British contribution was small – ships diverted to the region and one RAF squadron despatched – the British newspapers were keen to report that Mrs Thatcher, the veteran war leader, had 'put the backbone' into President Bush at the beginning of the crisis by reportedly telling him: 'This is no time to wobble, George.'

The steady president's Operation Desert Shield eventually included forces from Saudi Arabia, Morocco, Egypt and Syria. This local presence was vital to the American desire that the military operation should not be capable of interpretation as US colonialism or as a Christian holy war against

**Ashes to Ashes (2)** 1991
Oil, sand and collage on canvas
72 × 66 cm/28 × 26 in
Private Collection, UK

Islam. It was becoming increasingly clear that the new world order meant not an end to wars but subtle cultural changes in the methods of conducting them. In reality, though, America was in charge. The supreme commander of Operation Desert Storm was General Norman Schwarzkopf, a bull-necked and florid Floridian who, in the way of modern military top brass, was as skilled at press conferences as he was at battle strategy.

Only a few years after the events, most Britons have probably already forgotten the frenzied atmosphere of this phoney war period. Saddam Hussein's erratic behaviour – rounding up British residents of Kuwait in hotels, parading them before the cameras and then releasing them – prompted frequent newspaper comparisons with Adolf Hitler. Predictions of Armageddon were also common. It was widely believed that President Hussein would attack Israel with his own secret stock of nuclear weapons or that Israel would respond with nuclear weapons to a conventional attack. At best, a non-nuclear bloodbath was anticipated. Saddam Hussein had used chemical weapons against his own despised Kurdish population and the American Army, as well as issuing protective suits to all its troops, was also rumoured to have shipped thousands of 'body bags', for bringing home dead soldiers, to the Gulf. In Britain, there were rumours, as there had been during the Falklands, and almost certainly as false now as then, that call-up papers had been secretly printed.

John Keane remembers, during this period, shopping in Oxford Street when there was a power-cut: 'I thought how appropriate it was to the atmosphere of that time that there should be blackouts.'

Yet these moments of terror and tension during the pre-war period were punctuated by long periods in which it was possible to forget what was going on. Indeed, startlingly, the British Conservative Party took advantage of one such lull to remove from office Margaret Thatcher, prime minister for eleven years.

Although there would be officially no war in the Gulf until 15 January when the UN deadline passed – and General Schwarzkopf turned the defensive Operation Desert Shield into the offensive Operation Desert Storm – the Imperial War Museum in London decided in August 1990, immediately after the seizing of Kuwait, that it would spend £10,000 to send an official artist to the Persian Gulf.

John Keane recalls: 'There was a message from Angela Weight, at the Imperial War Museum, on my answerphone, saying something like: "How do you fancy being a chemical warfare victim?" And, I thought, well, you probably don't get asked this kind of thing twice, so I accepted straightaway . . .'

The Ministry of Defence, though, proved obstructive. This does not seem to have been a general philistine (or philistine general's) opposition to the idea of artists accompanying armies – for the MoD had made such arrangements in the Falklands and elsewhere – but rather a specific hostility to the idea of John Keane fulfilling the commission. The MoD said that they were unable to arrange insurance for the artist. Keane made inquiries about private cover but would have been required to pay £3,500 (or one third of his total fee) for a minimum £100,000 protection. Eventually, *The Guardian* newspaper arranged insurance for Keane and he was able to leave.

But, subsequently, in the Gulf, Keane met David Cobb, from the Royal Society of Marine Artists, whose request to paint watercolours from Royal Navy vessels had been accepted by the MoD without question and with a promise to provide him with insurance. The Ministry declines to explain this apparent discrepancy. 'You draw what conclusions you want,' says Keane, but it seems likely that the MoD had run a background check and disliked what it found. Keane was a member of both the CND and the Labour Party and had, of course, travelled to Northern Ireland and Nicaragua.

Once the problem of indemnity was settled, Keane was required to report to the Ministry of Defence in Whitehall to meet the press department. The artist recalls that he had to force his way through a group of anti-war protestors, including the CND chairman, Bruce Kent: an irony that Keane enjoyed.

The meeting, however, was brief and Keane received 'no training, no preparation, no briefing' before leaving for the Gulf except for a short session at an RAF base, where he took delivery of his 'Noddy suit', as the protective outfits against chemical weapons were known.

Historically, war art had fulfilled two purposes: the provision of a basic visual record in the years before the camera and the production of propagandistic images for the glory of the victors. In the latter connection, the Bayeux Tapestry is regarded by some as an early example of a rabble-rousing battle canvas. But the tradition of war art is generally thought to have begun in 1855, when the French artist Constantin Guys sent back wood-block engravings from the Crimean battlefront to the *Illustrated London News*. In 1916 the British government formally despatched the artist Muirhead Bone to the Western Front and it was during the 1914–18 conflict that the first wave of British war artists emerged. It included Paul Nash, Stanley Spencer, John Singer Sargent and C.R.W. Nevinson. Sargent's *Gassed* and Nash's *We Are Making a New World* – both trenchant trench images – are generally regarded as among the high points of the genre. During the Second World War, forty artists were commissioned by the War Ministry.

Nash and Sargent's work, for example, was not as jingoistic as the government might have hoped and so the propaganda aspect of war art was receding. Its task of reportage, however, was gradually being superseded by first the photograph and then by film. It was commonplace among students of culture that the Nashs, Sargents and Spencers of the Second World War, Vietnam and the Falklands worked for Pathé, Magnum, NBC, and the BBC. To these visual rivals of paint had now been added CNN, the American-based first-ever 24-hour cable news service, whose presence, and influence on other broadcasters, would make the 1991 Gulf War the first conflict to be a live television event.

John Keane – the Imperial War Museum's old-fashioned artistic howitzer against these super new visual weapons – felt untroubled by what many regarded as the redundancy of the project he was undertaking: 'Obviously you can't deny that the electronic media played a role in that war that superseded all previous wars, took on a new dimension. But the direction that they were going in was a totally different direction. News people are fulfilling a role that has to do with conveying information for tonight's news or tomorrow's breakfast table. In a way, I was liberated by that. I could try to redefine what being a war artist was. I didn't see my goal as perhaps a previous generation of war artists had. I didn't have to merely record what happened and I had no obligations to produce propaganda. In fact, I could address such questions as the political constraints on the other media. I saw myself as being outside all that. Quaint or not, I was able to be a bit of a maverick.'

But, as we have seen already, Keane's relationship as a painter with the rival visual forms is a complicated one: rather than ignoring electronic images, he borrows and mediates them. This approach triggered the first of the multiple controversies to afflict Keane on this project. The press and the public's romantic idea of a war artist demanded palette and oil paints in the kit-bag, the hunched figure working at the easel by the light of rocket glare. Keane – in accordance with the working methods that had served him in Nicaragua, Northern Ireland and Ollerton – took to the Gulf only a Camcorder and a reporter's notebook.

Keane is unrepentant about this method: 'For me, the camera is serving simply as a sketchbook of an instantaneous kind. Given that I want to make paintings – and paintings are essentially a reflective form, not an observational record, although they may contain elements of that – photography is simply the most practical way of recording information I may want to use later . . . a way of having information available to make a subsequent painting which is to do with the memory of that situation and having been in that situation.'

Armed with his Olympus sketchbook and his shorthand pads, Keane flew first to the RAF compound at Dahran. The only advantage of the MoD's lack of co-operation in Britain was that by the time Keane was cleared to travel, the war had become a real one. Operation Desert Storm had begun, with daily bombing raids of Baghdad and its neighbouring regions. Preparations for the ground offensive – to take back Kuwait – were beginning.

Keane went from Dahran to Bahrain, where the pilots and navigators of the Tornado bombers were requisitioned alongside the media. This situation made a vivid impression on the artist. Islamic restrictions on alcohol consumption meant that this was, to a large degree, the first officially dry war in the memory of most military and journalistic experts; but, in Bahrain, drinking was permitted, and hotels would be busy in the evenings: 'The pilots and navigators would be down in the bar drinking. They were in civvies and so you wouldn't necessarily know who was a journalist and who was air-crew until you suddenly caught sight of a pilot's watch or they said something. It was quite a bizarre experience, drinking with these people who were going out on bombing missions every day . . .'

The artist had the same accreditation and access as journalists but, unlike most individual journalists, was planning during his four-week stay to move between the RAF, the army and the navy. From Bahrain, he travelled deep into the Saudi desert, near the Iraqi border, to join the phalanx of news crews attached to the army's Forward Transmission Unit (FTU). He found a 'completely featureless landscape, in which the only feature was the military presence'. It was during this part of his stay that Keane experienced one of only two gas attacks he witnessed. On a press facility trip to a military hospital, the press's army minder suddenly ordered them to don their 'Noddy suits' because of a Scud attack on a nearby town. Never having practised dressing-drill, Keane was particularly bewildered and frightened by the emergency, which proved later to be a false alarm.

At this stage, with the ground war imminent, Keane was offered the choice of remaining with the FTU or taking one of the last helicopter flights out to join a ship in the Gulf, the planned next stage of his itinerary. Self-preservation played some part in the artist's decision to head for the sea: 'At least a couple of journalists had told me that it was widely expected that the media would be among the casualties in the next stage. I had no way of knowing it would turn into the rout it did . . .'

The ground war lasted exactly one hundred hours: a piece of symbolic stop-watching by President Bush. The attacking American alliance met little opposition, taking 23,500 Iraqi prisoners-of-war within the first two days, and the deaths among its own troops were very well within the military definition of 'acceptable losses'. Indeed, the worst British casualties of the operation – nine deaths – were victims of that chilling military euphemism 'friendly fire', killed when their tanks were accidentally taken out by American missiles.

The Iraqi Army was retreating northwards on the road to Basra, one of the towns nearest the border between Iraq and Kuwait. Apache helicopters were destroying retreating vehicles at will in an attack described by journalists as a 'turkey shoot'. It was after seeing pictures of charred trucks and corpses on the Basra road that President Bush halted the conflict, nervous of accusations of unnecessary savagery, despite a view among the American generals – as later reported in General Schwarzkopf's memoirs – that the Allies should continue on to Baghdad and depose or destroy President Hussein.

John Keane spent the hundred hours of the ground war frustratedly marooned on ships in the Gulf, redundant because Schwarzkopf had decided to advance on Kuwait solely by sand and not by sea. The artist's main memory is of unneeded doctors on hospital ships smoking and playing cards as news of the rout filtered through.

As soon as the war was over, he headed to Kuwait City, where he joined journalists inspecting the

**We Are Making a New World Order** 1991
Oil and mixed media on canvas
170.5 × 233 cm/67 × 92 in
Private Collection, UK

**Looking for Evidence (Shadows and Doubts in the Palace of Torture)** 1991
Oil and collage on canvas
174 × 231 cm/68½ × 91 in

evidence of the Iraqis' brutal occupation of the city. Keane also travelled to the Basra road, to see the remnants of the terror there. On the last morning of his trip, he had a few hours to fill before flying back to Dahran and then home, and went walking in Kuwait City. It was then that he took a series of colour photographs which would in due course make him a target for the British tabloid press.

Back in London, Keane worked for a year on the thirty-five paintings which would be exhibited in April 1992 at the Imperial War Museum as 'Gulf'. This sounds, superficially, like Keane's first simple, descriptive title for an exhibition but, on closer examination, the artist is still typically playing with words. The 'gulfs' between Western and Arab culture, between the battle-zones and the comfortable cities in which they appeared on television, and perhaps between what was reported and what actually happened are all invoked.

The artist was also handed by his subject a kind of structural pun. By working in his favourite medium, he was producing oil paintings of a war fought for oil. The title of one work, *Oil Painting*, makes the connection specific. As before, Keane also made frequent use of PVA and wax crayon, and collage materials of newspapers, Saudi and American bank-notes and pages from the Bible and the Koran. He incorporated sand as well; another structural pun, although the substance used was from a London building site.

*Before the War* was painted in Keane's period of limbo in London in late 1990 while waiting for MoD approval. A man and a woman are dancing in a field surrounded by trees. By lowering the perspective – a technique which, as we will see, would become frequent in his later work – he makes the figures giants. Their jeans and training shoes identify the couple with the West, and American influence, while the man's clenched fist and shadowed face add a hint of arrogance and sexual power to a theoretically carefree scene. An electricity pylon and the towers of a city beyond are perhaps a little pun on the idea of 'power', but also a reference to the complicated industrial structures which are about to be threatened by – and defended in – the war.

One of the works – *Laser-Guided*, in which a soldier is painting on a missile the slogan 'To Saddam, suck this, luv, Zelda' – is an accurate recreation of an image Keane captured with his camera, its title contrasting the so-called 'smart' technology of the new weaponry (laser-guided missiles were supposed to reduce the risk both to pilots in the air and civilians on the ground) with the primitive, jingoistic war-lust contained in the sub-sexual slogan. Here, the war artist boldly invites, or staunchly ignores, the question: why not a photograph?

In general, though, the canvases exploit the liberation that Keane felt himself to have from simple reportage. *Ecstasy of Fumbling (Portrait of the Artist in a Gas Alert)* features some of his most pointed use of collage. Another in Keane's line of mocking self-portraits, the picture derives from the emergency during the visit to a field hospital described above. The artist's terrified eyes glare out from the portholes of his gas-mask. But beneath the paint – and deliberately more legible than in most of Keane's collage work – are pages from *Survive to Fight*, the army's instruction manual on how to use a chemical protection suit. Diagrams explain the procedure for defecation: a function to which the wearers may well find themselves unusually prone. In the bottom left-hand corner are affixed a packet of Nerve Agent Pre-Treatment Tablets (a rather optimistic name for a hopeful antidote) and a detector paper for dangerous substances. On the other side of the canvas, a postcard of Sargent's *Gassed* makes a nod to both the history of war art and the history of chemical warfare.

*We Are Making a New World Order* also pays homage, in the title, to one of Keane's predecessors in the genre, Paul Nash, creator of the First World War painting, *We Are Making a New World*. At the extremities of the canvas stand a black American and, with his back to the artist, a Kuwaiti citizen. In the literal gulf between these representatives of discordant cultures, the khaki colour of sand is blackened with oil and other debris. A car – always an important presence in Keane's paintings, standing for technological beauty and ugly consumerism – here has greater symbolic weight than ever before: this red gas-guzzler is the Helen of Troy, the *casus belli*, of this particular conflict. In the distance fires rise. As in the Northern Ireland bonfire paintings, the flames may or may not be sinister. Oil fields normally show peaks of flame, but Saddam Hussein, in a desperate last gesture, torched the oil fields for which he had seized Kuwait in the first place. The border of the painting is pasted-down greenbacks: a touch which seems a return to the rougher, more openly agitprop, style of Keane's earlier work.

Somewhere between the approaches of cameraesque representation and polemical collage lie the works inspired by Keane's visits to Kuwait City and the Basra road in the days immediately after the cessation of the ground war.

*Looking for Evidence (Shadows and Doubts in the Palace of Torture)* shows a Kuwaiti police barracks (a former royal palace) which was believed to have been used by the occupying Iraqis as a detention and torture centre. In the debris strewn on the floor of the trashed palace, a single clear image stands out: a photograph of a young girl. Keane and the two British journalists he was accompanying found this snap lying on the floor and the artist photographed the photograph and subsequently affixed it to his picture. He found it poignant because nothing could be deduced about the identity of the girl.

On returning to London, Keane was surprised to see the photograph of the girl on the front of the magazine section of *The Independent on Sunday*. Inside was a long article by one of the journalists who had accompanied Keane, in which the girl's life and the circumstances that had brought her to the torture chamber were recreated in detail. Keane was amazed by this feat of research and the article is visible through the paint in the lower left-hand corner of the painting as another of Keane's sly references to the skills of modern journalism.

The nine works referring to the massacre on the road to Basra – six paintings titled *The Road to Hell* and three called *Ashes to Ashes* – show the artist completely abandoning representation for chaotic swirls and smears of paint, crayon, sand and coal. These paintings perhaps reflect the difficulty of finding a clear ideological line on this conflict. A war for oil, sneered one side. But oil is vital to the life you lead, riposted the other. Basra was an unjustified massacre, objects one pundit. Then why is Saddam still in power five years later? asks another. In Nicaragua, the Falklands and Ollerton Colliery, it had been easy to find a side to be on – or in Northern Ireland to treat both sides equally – but the Gulf was a moral and political quagmire and Keane's abstractionism in many of these paintings may be viewed as a response to this problem.

Certainly, it was the most specific of the canvases that got the artist into trouble. *Mickey Mouse at the Front* is a large, surreal seascape. Barbed wire curves round the coast at Kuwait City. In the distance, its skyscrapers rise. In the foreground are three startling images. On the left, a shopping trolley, stacked with missiles like monstrous cucumbers, scrunches with one of its wheels the Kuwaiti flag. In the centre, a madly grinning Mickey Mouse perches on some kind of plinth, which is surrounded by twists of shit. On the right, a palm tree, its trunk broken and buckled, bows down to the ground, like a camel drinking.

At the beginning of 1992, as early publicity for the forthcoming exhibition, Keane gave an interview to the London *Evening Standard*, which reproduced a number of paintings, including *Mickey Mouse at the Front*, and suggested that the stance of 'Gulf' would be anti-war, violently pacifistic. The telephone in Keane's Hackney studio began to ring as tabloid journalists indignantly followed up the story. The artist pretended to be someone else. That night, ambushed by reporters and photographers on the doorstep of his flat in Highbury, he again passed himself off as a friend of the artist, then sat inside with the lights off.

On Wednesday, 15 January, the *Mickey Mouse* painting appeared in *The Sun*, one of few modern art works to have been given this dishonour. The father of one of the British soldiers killed in the 'friendly fire' incident described above was quoted as saying: 'It's depraved.' Archie Hamilton, the Armed Forces minister, said: 'These pictures trivialise an important event.' The caption beneath a picture of the artist read 'Keane . . . handed £10,000', a phrase which suggested surreptitious transactions involving brown paper bags rather than a formal commission from a reputable museum. On another page, under the headline 'Black Art', a *Sun* editorial frothed:

*Two paintings of the Gulf War show Mickey Mouse sitting on a lavatory amid the destruction of Kuwait.*
*Families of dead soldiers are outraged at the sneer at their sacrifice.*
*We share their revulsion.*
*The painter, John Keane, was sent to the Gulf as an official war artist.*
*He is entitled to his opinions about the war.*
*But, feeling as he does, why did he accept the commission?*
*Just for the money?*

Keane's Falklands work had contained a number of references to *The Sun* but it had never occurred to him that the newspaper would contain references to him, and although he later came to the amused view that 'being the subject of an editorial in a paper selling four million copies a day was probably the high spot of my career', he initially found the experience dismaying.

The painting was being seriously misunderstood, both in general and in one vital specific. First, it was being generally assumed that the images in the picture were the malevolent inventions of a left-wing artist, but, in fact, each derived from the photographs Keane took on his last morning in the ruined Kuwait City. A supermarket had been used as an armoury by the Iraqis and there was a trolley stacked with missiles. And an amusement arcade had been commandeered by the invaders as a latrine. In the middle of it was a toddler's rocking toy of Mickey Mouse, around which human turds lay where they had fallen.

Hence – and *pace* the second misunderstanding – the Disney rodent was not sitting on a lavatory at all but rather on the plinth that was part of the toy. *The Sun*, and other newspapers, who interpreted it as a picture of Mickey Mouse (i.e. America) shitting symbolically on Kuwait were misreading the image. It, in fact, showed how the Iraqis had literally shat on Mickey Mouse.

Keane understood the possible symbolic interpretations of the figure – over the unauthorised use of which Disney briefly considered suing him – but insists that the reference was intended more widely: 'I was thinking of the American influence on Kuwait . . . on the "Mickey Mouse defences" of the Iraqis against an invasion from the sea that never came. But, above all, it was just a startling image that I had witnessed in that arcade.'

Here, perhaps, was evidence of one great disadvantage of war painting over photography: there was no easy way to distinguish between fact and imagination.

Keane's brush with controversy was not yet over. The Imperial War Museum decided that *Alien Landscape* – a desert landscape of a camouflaged tank that was bordered with thirty-four pages from a copy of the Koran the artist had found abandoned on the Basra road – should not be exhibited. Three years into the Iranian *fatwa* against Salman Rushdie, the museum feared Muslim reprisals against the

**Mickey Mouse at the Front** 1991
Oil on canvas
173 × 198 cm/68 × 78 in
Reproduced by permission of the Imperial War Museum, London

**Legacy** 1991
Oil on canvas
228.6 × 297.2 cm/90 × 117 in

painter for his appropriation of Islam's holy book. Later, when the exhibition stopped at Sheffield on its tour, the local council bowed to pressure from the Sheffield Council of Mosques and removed *Alien Landscape* and one of the *Road to Hell* canvases from public display, although they could be viewed in a private booth.

The artist's banned and tabloid-attacked paintings were evidence that war art can still make a political impact. As for artistic impact, Keane faced the problem of the later exponents of the genre. The single most famous visual image of the Gulf War, it would have to be admitted, was a photograph, taken by Neil Libbert for *The Observer*, of a charred corpse in a burnt-out jeep on the Basra road.

And yet even that photograph showed the difficulty of war art. To the uninformed viewer, the picture speaks of a rout, a massive and perhaps unjustified savagery. Within two years of the Gulf War, the three main international leaders who had begun the opposition to Saddam Hussein – Margaret Thatcher, George Bush and Mikhail Gorbachev – had all been forced out of power in political disgrace, while the defeated Hussein retained his presidency.

It is in the context of this paradox that Keane's 'Gulf' pictures make an eloquent case for their existence in the age of CNN. Canvases, they are saying, can capture the ambiguities, the mess, the chaos, the surrealism of war in a way that the camera never can.

**Every Time We Say Goodbye** 1991
Oil and video stills on canvas
128 × 143 cm/50 × 56 in

**Distant Shudder** 1991
PVA and crayon on paper
76 × 51 cm/30 × 20 cm
Private Collection, UK

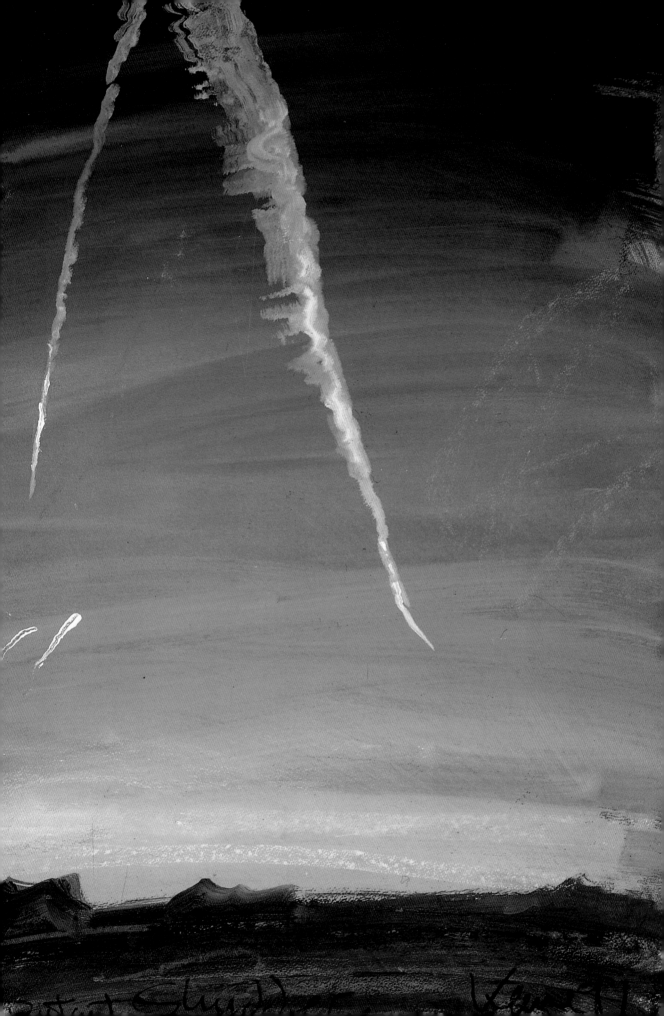

74

**Scenes on the Road to Hell (1)** 1991
PVA and crayon on paper
114.5 × 84 cm/45 × 33 in
Reproduced by permission of the
Imperial War Museum, London

**Laser-Guided** 1991
Oil on canvas
183 × 152.7 cm/72 × 60 in

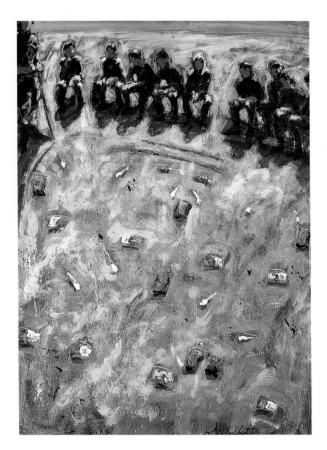

**Enemy** 1991
PVA and sand on paper
114.5 × 84 cm/45 × 33 in
Reproduced by permission of the
Imperial War Museum, London

**The Death Squad** 1991
Oil on canvas
203.5 × 173 cm/80 × 68 in
Reproduced by permission of the
Imperial War Museum, London

**El Basurero** 1992
PVA and collage on wood
152 × 76 cm/60 × 30 in
Private Collection, USA

# Human Rites
*Guatemala* 1992

FOR TWO YEARS, John Keane had been a kind of brush to hire – going to Ollerton Colliery and then the Gulf War at the invitation of others – and, after completing the Gulf paintings, his next body of work was again in response to an outside stimulus.

In 1991 Keane had joined a newly-founded group called the Association of Artists for Guatemala (AAG), becoming what he calls an 'affiliated luvvie' alongside actresses, theatre directors and journalists including Julie Christie, Charlotte Cornwell, Michael Bogdanov, Harold Pinter and Jill Tweedie.

In 1992 the group invited Keane to be one of the delegates on a fact-finding visit to the country, with a particular brief to examine economic hardship and human-rights abuses, in both of which areas the rulers of Guatemala were close to being world leaders.

Attracted by an organised tour after his frustrating freelance researches in Nicaragua, he agreed. Although he had been a neutral observer in Belfast, Ollerton and Saudi Arabia, Keane accepts that his stance on his trip was more partisan: 'Yes, it was. After working with the idea of the artist as outsider, it was interesting to be involved in something you believe is a good thing, are more actively committed to. Through what I do, I am obviously trying to influence people – I always have a line, however woolly that may be – but to actively align yourself with a cause, it was interesting to do that.'

Keane accepts that the eight-day trip, with its schedule and access controlled by others, was more superficial than his Nicaraguan project: 'a dip, really, rather than complete immersion'. He produced only ten canvases which, as well as being shown at the Flowers East gallery under the title 'Burden of Paradise', also illustrated a book of the same title published by the AAG containing the text of the delegation's report, written by Duncan Green.

Guatemala is the most populous state in Central America, with nine million inhabitants, and serves as a graphic illustration of the consequences of ancient Spanish conquest and modern political policing by the USA, which are the region's political inheritance.

A people's revolution in 1944 overthrew the so-called 'Liberal Dictatorship' which had ruled the independent country since 1871. The revolutionary governments introduced free elections, a minimum wage and agrarian reform to the coffee-exporting economy. The latter campaign included, in 1954, seizure of land belonging to the United Fruit Company, one of the American corporations which had become established in Guatemala since the late nineteenth century. In defence of the United Fruit Company, and accusing Guatemala of being a 'beachhead for Soviet expansion', the CIA organised the overthrow of the revolutionary government and installed a conservative régime which reversed most of the reforms.

Under these arrangements, economic inequalities intensified. By the late 1980s, it was calculated that more than 87 per cent of the nation lived below the poverty line, while two-thirds were too poor to purchase basic staples of food. This fiscal disparity is made worse by significant internal ethnic division. More than 50 per cent of the population is Mayan Indian, but this majority population is subject – in a Latin American equivalent of South African apartheid – to suppression, inequality and even organised extermination by the ruling class of 'Ladinos', who are mixed-race *mestizos*.

Although Guatemala's government has been technically a civilian one since 1985, the army has dominated politics since the counter-revolution of 1954. Revolutionary insurgency, which climaxed dramatically in the 1980s with rebellion in the highland areas populated by the Guatemalan Indians, has been brutally suppressed by the military through organised death squads. An estimated 440 villages were destroyed and up to 150,000 civilians murdered. In an attempt to prevent further unrest, the entire Guatemalan countryside was militarised with residence restricted to so-called 'model villages' under army surveillance. Insurgency continues, however, led by guerrillas of the URNG (Guatemalan National Revolutionary Unity).

At the time of the visit by the delegation that included Keane, it was the first year of the cosmetically civilian administration of President Serrano, elected theoretically democratically but on a very low turn-out against minimal opposition.

Many of Keane's small set of Guatemalan paintings were made on wood. 'It seemed appropriate,' he explains. 'The use of certain approaches – or materials – sometimes suggest themselves as being right for a subject. In this case, we'd visited a vast dump in Guatemala City in which people were scavenging for bits of wood. So it was to do with the notion of poverty, and the texture of life in a shanty town.'

One of the wood canvases, *El Basurero*, depicts the dump itself and therefore features another of the structural puns on which the artist is so keen. In this composition, too, his familiar collage technique achieves a thematic neatness, as a rubbish dump is itself a kind of collage, though created by random hands. If, in Keane's political paintings, the surface of old newspapers had a metaphorical aptness, here it has a literal one. The garbage across which a small boy is making his way has a three-dimensional reality.

According to the published report, it was the vast and teeming civic tip that made the most impression on the delegates. Surrounded by pigs and dogs on the ground and vultures in the air, the poor rootled through the stinking heap. And the dump features in a second of Keane's paintings, this time on paper and using crayon and collage, also called *El Basurero*, and showing the frenzied hunt for plunder among the rubbish, while huddles of vultures make their own surveillance of the garbage marketplace.

The most remarkable picture in this group, though, is *Base*, a fascinating further illustration of the difficulty raised by *Mickey Mouse at the Front*: establishing the difference in a more or less representational painting between the observed and the imagined. *Base* shows a huge pair of black army boots, topped by a massive camouflage helmet, around which are milling a number of peasants and some soldiers. Most uninformed viewers of the picture would surely assume that this was Keane's splendidly savage symbol for the militarisation of the rural parts of Guatemala.

But, in fact, the house-sized boots and hat are observed reality. In some kind of dark military nod at the story of Old Mother Hubbard, the army barracks in the Indian-populated town of Sololá is indeed built in this style. 'It was an astonishing thing,' recalls Keane. 'Like those hamburger stalls that are in the shape of a hamburger. Military justice in the shape of a boot!'

The other works are less polemical: scenes of normal domestic or professional existence amid the poverty and fear. *Ice-Cream in the Shanty Town*, another of the works on wood, makes a simple, touching opposition between the luxury treat for which three children are clamouring at a vendor's trolley, and the wretched functionality of the shanty shacks in which they live.

In *Burden of Paradise*, a man is stooped under the huge and unwieldy bushel of wood he carries on his back. This is one burden. The blazing sun – hinted at by the floppy sun-hat that completely obscures his face – is another. A makeshift cross on the grave suggests the third. But the palm trees, deep-blue lake and mountains in the distance confirm the title's claim that this is potentially a kind of paradise. For, as Keane remembers, 'one of the things that struck me in Guatemala was that, around

**Burden of Paradise** 1992
Oil on canvas
230 × 173 cm/90½ × 68 in

the poverty and terror, there was an unavoidable beauty. There was a picturesqueness about so much of it.'

The Guatemala pictures are angry – and many are politically specific – but there was no editorial in *The Sun*, no anguished debate at regional galleries about whether the exhibits could be shown. The reason for this, of course, was, ironically, the perception that AAG and its delegation had attempted to redress: that nobody cared about Guatemala. Certainly, no one could accuse the artist of having cashed in on the notoriety – and resulting greater bankability – that the Gulf assignment had brought him.

**Ice-Cream in the Shanty Town** 1992
Oil on wood
90 × 83 cm/35½ × 32½ in
Private Collection, France

**Before You Get to the Dump** 1992
PVA on wood
49 × 73.5 cm/19 × 29 in

**Supping with the Devil** 1993
Oil on canvas
203 × 211 cm/80 × 83 in

# Turning off the Television
## *London Life* 1993

THERE IS a well-documented phenomenon of soldiers and journalists who return from wars finding themselves alienated from their home country, which seems disturbing and imperfect in a way it never did before. No matter how many inoculations the traveller has, it seems, they still come back jaundiced.

Something of this seems to have afflicted Keane after his two years of work on the Gulf War and Guatemala. Turning his eyes again to the London in which he lived, he produced his bleakest, most troubling and most grimly sardonic group of works. It is also perhaps significant that he had been looking at a lot of Goya's work before beginning.

'The Struggle for the Control of the Television Station', an exhibition which showed in New York in April 1993 and at Flowers East in June, comprised fifteen paintings; eleven oil on canvas and four using PVA and crayon on paper.

The title refers to the first act of revolutionaries or armies in a modern coup or civil war: to seize the broadcasting centre in order to control the flow of information and propaganda. Examples of this tactical manoeuvre had been seen in the disintegrating Soviet Union and the former Yugoslavia in the period immediately before Keane began work.

But the title has a Western resonance as well as an Eastern one. 'I was interested in the glamour and power of television in all societies,' says Keane. 'If you want to exert influence or gain power, there's nothing as sexy as doing it through that particular channel – if you'll excuse the expression.'

Since the mid-1980s, the business strategy of Rupert Murdoch had been, increasingly, to expand beyond newspapers into television: through his Sky satellite station and the creation of Fox Television, a fourth major terrestrial network in the USA. Rival magnates such as Conrad Black and Viscount Rothermere also had their eye on the screen. Simultaneously, an ideological battle was taking place between the Conservative government and the liberal broadcasting establishment over the future of British television and, in particular, the funding and structure of the BBC. Therefore, the words 'The Struggle for the Control of the Television Station' were, at this time in history, by no means apposite only to desperate mustachioed generals aiming their tanks at some makeshift broadcasting HQ in a shanty town.

Appropriately enough, the germ of the works was in Germany, where East and West met. The earliest painting in the set, *Humiliation of the Ideologue on the Road to Freedom*, dating from 1990, was Keane's response to the fall of the Berlin Wall in 1989: the beginning of the collapse of communist Eastern Europe. A naked and probably dead man – the 'ideologue' of the title and, presumably, an old politician – lies slumped in a cruciform position in a shopping trolley in which he has been dumped. The receptacle is, presumably, a variation on Trotsky's 'dustbin of history'.

Keane is not simplistically lamenting the end of communism, but rather dramatising the startling way in which a hugely powerful political ideology can suddenly be thrown away and values to which minds and lives have been devoted for decades become meaningless. Implicit in this is a reference to the speed with which alternative ideas can be taken up. The painting was made at a time of substantial capitalist triumphalism in the West. Both Margaret Thatcher and President George Bush made speeches about the 'victory of the West' over communism and a modish American bestseller, *The End of History* by Francis

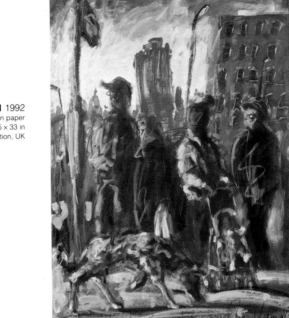

**Fear at the Bus Stop II** 1992
PVA and wax crayon on paper
114 × 84.5 cm/45 × 33 in
Private Collection, UK

**Fear at the Bus Stop** 1992
Oil on canvas
206 × 163 cm/81 × 64 in

Fukayama, argued that the history of ideas was effectively over because free market economics had so decisively won the argument.

In fact, the capitalist West was about to enter a terrible recession, the electoral victims of which would include both Thatcher and Bush. This historical irony is at the heart of the 'Television Station' paintings, in which the West – or, at least, London, one of its proud capitals – looks anything but triumphant.

Although still somewhat journalistic in approach, these canvases are more allegorical than Keane's earlier work. Apart from the television-set itself, which looms in three of the works, these paintings are dominated by two symbolic images. The first has been around since painters first lived, and, more particularly, died: the skeleton and the skull. It may be relevant here that the artist's father, Granville Keane, had died in Harpenden from cancer, aged eighty-five, while his son was preparing to leave for the Gulf. The death of a parent generally turns the thoughts of their children towards mortality, and these canvases are in part another example of the process.

The other recurring symbol is Keane's own coinage: the shopping trolley. A traditionalist art historian might consider that in comparison with bleached bones – standing for the ancient and constant human fear of death – a supermarket cart lacks symbolic resonance, but this would be a fundamental misunderstanding of shopping trolleys.

A shopping trolley, by its very size, implies voracious and careless consumption; the poor and frugal choose the much smaller baskets on offer. Shopping trolleys were originally an American invention and were a response to the famed range of items on offer to US consumers in what were first supermarkets and then hypermarkets. And the astonishing spread of comestibles in these food emporia – so many cheeses, so many meats, so many breakfast cereals – itself had a political undercurrent. This capitalist cornucopia was a deliberate visual rebuke to communism. In Russia there were bread queues, but, in America, the buyers needed shopping trolleys to carry all their loaves away. Each of these deep, wheeled hoppers was a declaration that the US economy was not a basket-case.

Already trailing these rich economic associations, the shopping trolley has developed, in Britain, further reverberations. Supermarket carts live a strange urban counter-life. Anyone who has ever pushed one suspects that they have a mind of their own – the wheels notoriously curve out the reverse of any turn requested of them – and this perception is confirmed by their fabled wanderings.

Vaguely sinister even in their proper shopping environment – Dalek-like in their skeletal silveriness – they are regularly stolen, or steal away, at night and are used in races, hurled from bridges and tower blocks or simply left abandoned by the roadside miles from home. So serious did the problem of itinerant shopping trolleys become that, in the Environment Protection Act of 1990, a clause was included permitting local councils to impound stray carts and charge the supermarkets for their return. (There is also an internal reference, for a shopping trolley loaded with missiles was one of the elements in the controversial *Mickey Mouse at the Front*.)

The title work of the set, *The Struggle for the Control of the Television Station,* is a kind of quasi-altarpiece featuring four panels and a predella. The top panel would, in a conventional altarpiece, usually feature a representation of God or the heavens. Keane's celestial canopy is dominated by a man-made dweller on high: a broadcasting satellite. The bottom panel returns to earth, and about as low as you can go, with a representation of London's Cardboard City, in which a homeless person not only has no television in their house but is making their home in a television packing box: it is clearly marked 'Sony'.

Similar ironies of production and consumption are played out across the two side panels. Both feature glowing electronic screens, but, on the left, they are the laptops and terminals of editorial input by hunched journalists; while, on the right, they are the screens and cathode-rays of editorial output to slumped teenagers. What goes around comes around, as the Americans say. The blacks and blues the artist has used lay a sepulchral gloom over these scenes.

The central panel is less representational: a sinister collage of exaggerated images. A baseball-capped man, accompanied by a young boy in plastic Mickey Mouse ears, tips dollars from a briefcase into a shopping trolley pushed by a blindfolded skeleton. In the middle-ground, a naked man lies slumped and twisted in a shopping trolley, and a man holds a knife to the throat of another. Elsewhere, sophisticates, in safe pools of warm domestic light, sip drinks or eat a meal. Outside the televison station, a vast crowd is being addressed by a man whose raised crucifix seems to identify him as an evangelist. Together, the five panels offer a tableau of the users and the used, the powerful and powerless, in the technocracy of modern life.

The title work replays, or offers close-ups of, moments from the other fourteen paintings. The dinner-party motif, for example, is at the heart of *Supping with the Devil*, another of the large oils. At a white-clothed table bearing roses and champagne, clear representatives of that derided '90s group, 'the chattering classes', are, as they say, 'putting the world to rights'. But they are, in a favourite Keane image, comfortably protected from that world. Outside the windows, the city is dark and ominous. The artist himself stands beside the table, holding a portable phone, in a jokey allusion to Dix's 1922 painting *To Beauty*, in which the artist holds an old Bakelite receiver. Around the edge of the painting are placed icons of new technology: a fax machine, a camera crew, a TV reporter, the screens of journalists and City dealers.

The picture is reminiscent of Harold Pinter's 1992 play *Party Time*, in which a swish drinks party is conducted in a smart apartment, while some kind of military crackdown takes place on the streets below. Keane, like Pinter (an admirer and buyer of the artist's work), seems disturbed by the ease with which the urban middle classes can close their minds to unpleasant realities, despite surrounding themselves with state-of-the-art sources of information from the world. The point is made more explicitly in *Death at the Next Table*, in which an urgent television in a corner is ignored by nearly all the diners in a restaurant.

*Supping with the Devil* acknowledges, both visually and through the title, Keane's complicity in the world he is satirising. Indeed, this may go even further than the viewer of the painting suspects. Probably the majority of Keane's friends work in the media world, including the comedian Alexei Sayle, the television presenter Angus Deayton and the literary agent Cat Ledger.

The rest of the paintings in the sequence go out onto the streets, where the predominant mood is menace, fear and an atmosphere of regret and neglect that the novelist Martin Amis has called 'street sadness'. Indeed, these works feel like a visual analogue to Amis's London novels: Keane had read *Money* (1984) and greatly admired it. Equally, you could easily imagine one of these paintings as the illustration on the sleeve of an Elvis Costello song like 'A Kinder Murder' or 'Fifteen Steps to Hell'. Like Costello's songs and Amis's novels, they are part of a strain in contemporary culture which depicts London as a cruel, brooding and sinister city.

In *Metropolitan Love*, for example, Keane takes a traditional romantic image – a man and woman embracing under a street-light – and renders it weird and threatening. The perspective is the equivalent of what is known in television as a 'pavement shot', in which the positioning of the camera at ground level exaggerates the size of foreground images in relation to background ones. Keane's lovers are nearly as tall as the lamp-post, at least twice the size of the house and car in the rear of the composition. A dog at their feet becomes rat-sized. These casual snoggers loom over London like King Kong.

In *Shopping*, a skeleton pushes a supermarket trolley laden with unidentified objects under a darkly smeared sky. It is a terrifying image. This ghoul, you suspect, is the 'First Shopper of the Apocalypse', the modern commercial world's successor to the Four Horsemen as an omen of doom. There is also a kind of visual pun on the subject of skeletons: unlike a bag or a box, a shopping trolley is skeletal, looking more like the middle of an object than an object itself.

A trio of linked canvases, *Fairy Tales of London I, II and III*, dramatise oppression and pressure. In the first, a woman walks across a London wasteland, bowed, like a Mother Courage of the Sainsburys age, under a shopping trolley, in which one child sits while another, walking, tugs at her hand. She is about to step over a skull. The second *Fairy Tale* shows a young man in jeans and sneakers bent under a trunk or skip. The 'pavement-shot' perspective is employed again so that he is larger than a house or car. The third *Fairy Tale* features a similarly-burdened man hauled forward by a huge Alsatian. There is a supermarket cart in the foreground, and someone has been shopping for skulls again.

For Keane, the *Fairy Tale* series, with their variously burdened persons, concern 'psychological and emotional baggage rather than anything more directly political. I accept that many people do see them politically, because they're clearly about oppression of some kind.'

A series of works on the theme of urban anxiety – a world in which no one can feel safe – ends, fittingly enough, with a painting invoking the totemic modern horror: the murder of the toddler Jamie Bulger by two ten-year-olds in a Mersey shopping-mall in February 1993. In *Child with Skull*, a young boy is playing soccer with Yorick, kicking the dead-head contemptuously along the ground.

After years of work with its eye turned away from London, Keane was acknowledging that lack of charity may begin at home.

**The Humiliation of the Ideologue on the Road to Freedom** 1990
Oil on canvas
216 × 163 cm/85 × 64 in

**Fairy Tales of London 1** 1992
Oil on canvas
206 × 163 cm/81 × 64 in
Collection: Hull City Museums, Art Galleries and Archives

**Fairy Tales of London 2** 1992
Oil on canvas
206 × 163 cm/81 × 64 in

**The Struggle for the
Control of the Television
Station** 1992
Oil on canvas
Centre panel:
198 × 198 cm/78 × 78 in
Left and right panels:
198 × 91.5 cm/78 × 36 in
Top panel: 38 × 91 cm/15 × 36 in
Bottom panel: 68.5 × 198 cm/27 × 78 in

**Shopping** 1993
Oil on canvas
51 × 40.5 cm/20 × 16 in
Private Collection, USA

**Child with Skull** 1992
Oil on canvas
51 × 41 cm/20 × 16 in
Private Collection, USA

**Metropolitan Love**
Oil on canvas
51 × 40.5 cm/20 × 16 in
Private Collection, UK

**Choice** 1993
Oil on canvas
51 × 40.5 cm/20 × 16 in
Private Collection, UK

# Burning Issues
## *Fire Paintings* 1994

IMAGES OF flames had flickered in the background of both the Northern Ireland and the Gulf paintings. The symbol of the ideological or demagogic mob had swarmed through the 'Television Station' canvases. In the series of paintings which Keane produced during 1994, these two concerns merged.

In another twist on the relationship between the artist's work and rival visual media, the paintings exhibited at the Riverside Studios in November 1994 under the title 'Fear of God' sprang from an advertisement. The Italian-run clothing company Benetton became notorious in 1993 with a series of commercials deliberately calculated to shock readers and viewers and thus attract publicity to the company. One featured a photograph taken at the death bed of a victim of Aids. Another showed the blood-stained uniform of a soldier who had died during the civil war, which began in April 1992, in Bosnia-Herzegovina, one of the uneasily independent republics formed from the litter of the communist Yugoslavia. A third controversial Benetton advertisement featured a burning car. This was the one that triggered the imagination of John Keane.

'As an image it interested me,' he remembers. 'The notion of human ingenuity being dispensed with by the power of nature – inflamed for whatever reason.'

The conflicts in the former Yugoslavia – which shattered any fantasies that still remained after the Gulf War of a new world order – were another strong influence on the gestation of these paintings. The Serbian attacks on Bosnia-Herzegovina – and the intransigence of all sides in the conflict – were, for Keane, another illustration of the nationalism and fundamentalism which had surfaced in the Gulf, the former Soviet Union and even in the rise of the intolerant religious-political Right in American politics, which was echoed in Britain by John Major's ruinous 'Back to Basics' campaign, which was supposed to be the restoration of traditional and moral values but which led to the regular undermining of his government by sex scandals.

'I became interested in the idea of destruction wrought in the name of religion,' Keane recalls. 'Or, rather, more generally, faith, because faith can be political as well. I think I was addressing in a rather dark way – because these are rather dark and oppressive paintings – what manifests itself in fundamentalism. They're very much post-Cold War paintings, because I was also concerned with the death of a political notion of progress, tolerance, pluralism, liberalism – things that I believe in and value and which led me foolishly to believe that humanity was advancing, improving . . .'

Keane contemplated, in his now established go-and-show approach, travelling to Bosnia to explore these themes. But the Imperial War Museum soon appointed Peter Howson to the role Keane had filled in the Gulf and he felt that it would be wrong to introduce a kind of market competition to the artistic chronicling of the conflict. There was also, as he admits, the less morally elevated objection that he was 'frankly bloody scared'. The war in Bosnia was a bloody free-for-all in comparison with the unequal match in the Gulf. Like his Falklands paintings of twelve years before, but with the refinements of method and message which had accrued in that time, these works would be created from a distance and rely on images provided by other media.

Working on the paintings, Keane became more and more obsessed with images of conflagration and himself always refers to these works as the 'Fire Paintings' rather than by their official exhibition title.

**Home** 1994
Oil and sand on canvas
51 × 40.5 cm/20 × 16 in

**Fear of God**
1994
Oil and sand on
canvas
226 × 249 cm/
89 × 98 in

**Pig Supper**
1993
Oil on canvas
223.5 × 244 cm/
88 × 96 in

He was interested in both the use of burning as a method of destruction during war or revolution and in the religious associations of flames: the 'divine spark', the depiction of the Holy Spirit as tongues of flame, the 'purgatorial fires' and the flames of Hell.

The Bosnian conflict – which was reported nightly on the BBC and CNN during its early stages but in which the West made no intervention beyond support for a United Nations peace-keeping force – could be seen as another example of the 'compartmentalisation' or easy indifference which had been a central theme of Keane's work since the beginning. Two of the paintings explicitly pick up the symbol of the ignorant or blinkered dinner-party employed in the 'Television Station' set.

Several of the pieces share the title *Dark Ages*, which Keane intends as a reference to 'the fact that we may be flattering ourselves as a civilisation – that we're not out of the dark ages yet'. Three of these pictures – *Car, Home* and *Bus* – are simple single-image variations on the idea which was the project's visual starting-point: the destruction of new technology by the primal force of fire.

The two vehicles and a building burn against a background of streaks of black paint smeared roughly against dollar bills. Apart from money, Keane collaged into these creations pages of the New Testament, the Jewish Bible, the Communist Manifesto and – despite, or perhaps because of, his troubles in Sheffield over 'Gulf' – tearings from the Koran. The only light in these dark compositions – their style underlining another meaning of the title – is provided by the ruinous illumination of flames. *Home* was based on a picture Keane freeze-framed from a television news bulletin – a technique he sometimes uses for source material – of a house ablaze in Sarajevo, as part of the Serbian policy of so-called 'ethnic cleansing'.

In *Dinner in the Ruins*, a sleek meal is taking place but the chattering friends are unaware of, or at best uninterested in, the blazing skyscrapers of a torched city behind them. In the bottom left corner, the child with skull from the 'Television Station' pictures boots his cruel football across the wasteland. In *Pig Supper*, another dinner-party gorges itself on pork, while images of wealth (a leafy country house with smart cars outside) and devastation (another blazing city) provide a literal frame of references from Keane's earlier work, and particularly from the last major set of paintings. Some viewers may see *Pig Supper* as political – thinking, perhaps, of the reference at the end of Orwell's *Animal Farm* to the faces of humans and pigs around a table being indistinguishable – but, according to the artist, its inspiration came from his own vegetarianism. Its principal target is meat-eaters rather than political or class carniverousness.

This collection breaks down into clusters of paintings exploring sub-themes. A trio of canvases, for example, are based around the symbol of the mob or crowd.

In *Fear of God*, the bottom of the picture holds a pack of fixed and angry faces, while the rest is filled with another conflagration of skyscrapers. The implication is that the destruction has occurred as a result of their devotion to the cause that fires them up. The title is a typical pun: this group of piously violent people is inspired by reverential fear of its God, but is now, in the English colloquial phrase, 'putting the fear of God' into the rest of the population.

*Grace of God*, another study of a burning building, plays the same language game. The people who committed this terrible act believe themselves filled with God's grace but, again in the idiomatic expression, it is only 'the grace of God' that spares each of us from such a fate and, a third meaning, there is the eternal question of why a deity would allow his grace to be exercised in such a violent way.

Similarly, the crowd of ecstatic faces that fills the whole of the canvas in *One Voice* listens to a single voice – that of its God or demagogue – and subsequently comes to speak with a single tongue, but is unwilling to accept that, in a pluralistic society, it represents only 'one voice' among many. This painting, however, is more careful and detailed in its representation than most of these 1993–94 works.

Each head has a halo of orange light around it, from a fire behind it, and there is also, in the pile of heads that forms the baying mob, surely a deliberate visual echo of the horrific stacks of human skulls which have been discovered following massacres in Uganda, Cambodia and, more recently, Rwanda.

It is not merely because of the many flashbacks to the most recent set of pictures that these canvases have the feeling of transitional work. Keane was deliberately experimenting again with a rougher style, distressing the surface of the painting with sand or collage. The resulting paintings have the feeling of a low-key coda to the large and sophisticated achievements of 'The Struggle for the Control of the Television Station'.

Perhaps part of the problem was that, for the first time since the Falklands pictures, the artist was working from second-hand visual material, rather than a location or atmosphere he had personally experienced. And so, after completing them, he made another of his journeys.

**Renouncing Violence** 1994
PVA and crayon on paper
114 × 84.5 cm/45 × 33 in
Private Collection, UK

**Dark Ages (Bus)** 1994
PVA, sand and collage on paper
114 × 84.5 cm/45 × 33 in

**Dark Ages (Car)** 1994
PVA, sand and collage on paper
114 × 89 cm/45 × 35 in

**Dark Ages (Home)** 1994
PVA, sand and collage on paper
114 × 84 cm/45 × 33 in

**Untitled (Grace of God)**
1994
Oil and sand on canvas
159 × 127 cm/62½ × 50 in

**Dinner in the Ruins** 1993
Oil and mixed media on canvas
229 × 246 cm/90 × 97 in

**One Voice** 1994
Oil and sand on canvas
142 × 167.5 cm/56 × 66 in

**Todos Somos Marcos** 1995
PVA, collage and oil stick on paper
114 × 84 cm/45 × 33 in

# The Heat in Greeneland
## *Mexico* 1995

THE IDEA OF the 'film of the book' – a work of literature being visually interpreted on celluloid – is well established. John Keane's project for 1995, though, pursued the more unusual idea of the 'paintings of the book'. Throughout the year, he worked on a number of canvases and smaller works on paper which were shown at Flowers East in November 1995 under the title 'Graham Greene and the Jungle of Human Dilemma'.

The easy critical response to these works would be that Keane, the modern painter with the largest collection of Air Miles, the Passport Artist, had clocked up another country, and, moreover, a further territory in the Americas. But, in fact, the pictures were far more serendipitous. During the previous year, the artist had been feeling 'rather bleak and miserable, for various reasons' – a mood which, he accepts, had permeated the 'Fire Paintings' – and was glad to begin 1995 with a month's holiday, accompanying his partner, the television producer Rosemary McGowan, to Mexico, where she was visiting a friend.

Keane had no intention to research or work during the visit, but the creatively inclined often find that their ideas-box has smuggled itself into the luggage even when they pointedly left it at home. He found himself increasingly fascinated by a country in the grip of extreme political instability following the signing during 1994 of the North American Free Trade Agreement, which tied Mexico economically to its northern neighbours, the USA and Canada. The leading opposition candidate for president had been assassinated on the campaign trail and there had been an uprising by the Zapatista guerrillas, led by Subcommandante Marcos, an enigmatic latter-day Che Guevara. Unrest had led to a 'peso crisis', with America's President Clinton pumping in dollars in the hope of keeping the currency afloat.

Keane travelled around the country, using the apartment of his partner's friend in Mexico City as a base, and, during his last weekend there, he discovered around in the flat a copy of Graham Greene's 1938 non-fiction work, *The Lawless Roads*, an account of his travels through Mexico investigating the suppression of Catholicism being carried out during that period by the socialist government, including the execution of many priests. Greene would subsequently draw on the same material in his celebrated 1940 novel, *The Power and the Glory*, also set in Mexico.

Reading *The Lawless Roads*, in January 1995, Keane was startled by the discovery that his own itinerary in Mexico had almost exactly matched Greene's from fifty-seven years before. This similarity stretched even to the fact that Greene had been reading Trollope's *Barchester Towers* on his trip, which was exactly the holiday reading packed six decades later by Keane's partner.

Greene and Keane had rhyming names and chiming preoccupations, but there was also a deeper connection between them. Initially, the artist's connection with the novelist had been merely the standard one of reader to writer. When Keane was thirteen, his older brother had given him a copy of *The Quiet American*, Greene's Vietnam novel. 'He fascinated me as a writer and an individual,' the artist recalls. 'I never related to the Catholic element at all. I think, initially, it was because there's something about the air of desolation and seediness in his novels that appeals particularly to teenage adolescents. After that, it was identification with certain parts of the world – Nicaragua, Panama – that appealed to me. The idea that he, as an artist, could be involved in that way . . .'

**Endangered Species** 1995
PVA, collage and oil stick on paper
114 × 84 cm/45 × 33 in

Artistic engagement with politics was the cause of an intriguing communication between the two men. Knowing of Greene's enthusiasm for the Sandinistas in Nicaragua, Keane wrote to the novelist in 1988, enclosing a set of transparencies of the 'Bee-Keeping in the War-Zone' paintings, and asking whether he might provide an introduction to the catalogue. In a letter dated 22 December 1987 – on the headed notepaper of his exile's flat in the Avenue Pasteur in Antibes – the novelist replied:

> Thank-you very much for sending me the photos of your pictures of Nicaragua. I like them immensely . . . May I keep the transparencies, even though I am afraid I can't offer to do the introduction. The trouble is that at 83 one finds one's time running short and there is more and more to do . . .

At that stage of Keane's career, transparencies represented a significant expense and he wrote to Greene politely requesting their return. A second letter from the Avenue Pasteur, dated 20 January 1988, explained:

> I am desolated that I didn't realise that you wished to have your photographs back. I was discussing them with a friend abroad, who very much wanted to see them, and I posted them to him. I am afraid abroad in this case was Russia. I am writing to try and recover them but the posts both ways are very hazardous.

Greene was well known to have one particular friend who lived in Russia – the former spy, Kim Philby – and Keane has always wondered whether his Nicaraguan transparencies were found in the clutter of Philby's KGB grace-and-favour apartment in Moscow after the death of the great traitor. Certainly, it remains very possible that – as well as being the only artist of his generation to have been the subject of a *Sun* editorial – Keane is the only one to have been the subject of a telephone conversation between Graham Greene and Kim Philby.

In early 1995, back from his month in Mexico, the artist began the process that would lead to Keane and Greene coming together over another set of transparencies, though in a very different – and, for the novelist, posthumous – relationship. As was his habit, he worked first on paper, creating images which would be built up into the larger canvases. As often before, he used collage materials – pages of a Spanish bible, Mexican newspapers – although, the trip not having been organised for research purposes, he was working from fewer photographs than had been the case with the formal projects involving abroad. Keane also experimented in terms of method, using for the first time 'oil sticks' (a kind of crayon of oil paint) and mixing beeswax with the paint to thicken and ridge it on the canvas.

The title work, *Graham Greene and the Jungle of Human Dilemma*, is an altarpiece similar to the title painting in the 'Television Station' set, though consisting of only three panels. The left-hand panel is based around the church in the Mayan Indian village of San Juan Chamula, visited by both Greene and Keane. It also includes the juxtaposed images, in reality separated by more than half a century, of Greene in his sun-hat and tropical suit, taken from a photograph illustrating his travel book, and of the white Volkswagen car in which Keane later travelled in preference to the mule that had been used by the writer. Two dogs copulating in the dust provide a classically Greenian – though also Keanian – image of bleakness.

The right-hand panel features the clerical executions which were the focus of Greene's book. In the background, Padre Pro, the most famous of the dissident Mexican priests, faces a firing squad, his arms outstretched like Christ's on the cross. In the foreground, an anonymous priest is being hanged.

The central panel is an expanse of jungle, in which some more or less expected items – a brilliant

**Edge of the Jungle** 1995
Oil and beeswax on canvas
228 × 218 cm/90 × 86 in

toucan, a sinister monkey with an erect penis – and some unlikely ones have been placed side by side to make a surreal landscape. There is one of the dolls of Subcommandante Marcos – complete with miniature ammo belt, machine-gun and face scarf – which are a popular Mexican novelty. There is a computer terminal, a familiar Keane image for at least fifteen years, and here a reference to the way in which the country's guerrillas now use the Internet (the worldwide computer link) for propaganda purposes.

The Internet guerrilla is also tapping away at his terminal in *Edge of the Jungle*, another of the large works, which continues Keane's strain of self-deprecating self-portraits. The artist, in baseball cap and shades, wanders through the rain forest at Palenqué, looking as incongrous as a tourist in a war-zone might. 'It's a completely made-up scene,' explains Keane. 'But the idea was the incongruity of tourism, seeking pleasure and relaxation against a background of such grim realities. The self-consciousness I feel on such occasions isn't all-consuming, but I can't entirely banish it, this sense of being an imposter.'

But, for all Keane's continuing unease about art and his own capabilities, it seemed likely that the Mexican set – including later paintings concerning Mexico's modern history – would prove another successful stop on Keane's world tour.

And, while he produced images based on Graham Greene's words, Keane was contemplating a temporary move into television, planning a documentary on the Americas, based around the image of the Pan-American Highway. Another rival form had been embraced; another conflict of interest exposed or resolved.

La Residence des Fleurs.
Avenue Pasteur.
06600 Antibes

22nd December 1987

Dear Mr Keane,

Thank you very much for sending me the photos of your
pictures of Nicaragua.  I like them immensely.  Perhaps
the one I like best of all is The Road from Esteli.  May
I keep the transparencies even though I am afraid I cant
offer to do the introduction.  The trouble is that at
83 one finds one's time running short and there is more
and more to do.  I dont think I have a clear moment
before February and even then difficulties may arise.
One of my troubles is that I am struggling hard to
finish an unsatisfactory novel before the end comes.
I think I would hesitate in any case because a writer
finds it difficult to express his opinion of paintings.
Literary criticism comes easily but one feels one's
ignorance when one starts trying to describe a painting
or to appreciate a painting.  Do forgive me.

Yours sincerely

La Résidence des Fleurs.
Avenue Pasteur.
06600 Antibes

20th January 1988

Dear John Keane,

I am desolated that I didn't realise that
you wished to have the photographs back.  I was
discussing them with a friend abroad who very
much wanted to see them and I posted them to him.
I am afraid abroad in this case was Russia.  I am
writing to try and recover them but the posts both
ways are very hazardous.  Do you want these new
transparencies back?  I really am very sorry for this
mistake.

With all good wishes for the catalogue.
Yours sincerely

**Letters from Graham Greene to the artist, 1988**

**Zapatista Jungle** 1995
PVA, oil stick and collage on paper
114 × 84 cm/45 × 33 in

**The Fat American Tourist and the Banana Tree** 1995
PVA and wax crayon on paper
114 × 84 cm/45 × 33 in

**Graham Greene and the Jungle of Human Dilemma** 1995
PVA, collage and oil stick on paper
114 × 84 cm/45 × 33 in

**Graham Greene and the Jungle of Human Dilemma** 1995
Oil on canvas
Centre panel: 228.5 × 200.5 cm/90 × 79 in
Side panels: 198 × 91.5 cm/78 × 36 in

# BIOGRAPHY OF THE ARTIST

1954    Born Hertfordshire
1972–76  Camberwell School of Art

## Solo Exhibitions

1980    'Peking, Moscow, Milton Keynes',
        Minsky's Gallery, London
1982    'Some of it Works on Paper', Centre
        181, London
1984    'War Efforts', Pentonville Gallery,
        London
1985    'Conspiracy Theories', Angela Flowers
        Gallery, London
        'Perspective 1985', Basel Art Fair,
        Switzerland
1986    'Work Ethics', Angela Flowers Gallery,
        London
1988    'Bee-Keeping in the War-Zone',
        Angela Flowers Gallery, London
        'Against the Wall', Turnpike Gallery,
        Leigh, Greater Manchester
        'The Accident', commissioned painting
        and screenprint for Greenpeace,
        Flowers East, London
1989    'Divided States', Terry Dintenfass
        Gallery, New York
        Forum, Hamburg, Germany
1990    'The Other Cheek?' Flowers East,
        London
1991    'Cloth Caps and Hang-Gliding' Angel
        Row Gallery, Nottingham
        'The Other Cheek?', Arts Council
        Gallery, Belfast
        'Before the War', Kelvingrove Art
        Gallery, Glasgow
1992    'Gulf', Imperial War Museum,
        London; Northern Centre for
        Contemporary Art, Sunderland;
        Graves Art Gallery, Sheffield; Tullie
        House, Carlisle; Aberdeen Art Gallery,
        Aberdeen
        'Fairy Tales of London', Lannon Cole
        Gallery, Chicago
        'Burden of Paradise', Flowers East at
        London Fields, London

        'Not the Gulf', Watermans Arts
        Centre, London
1993    'The Struggle for the Control of the
        Television Station', Terry Dintenfass
        Gallery, New York; Flowers East,
        London
        'Gulf', Norton Gallery, Palm Beach,
        Florida
1994    'The Struggle for the Control of the
        Television Station', Galerie
        Leuenberger, Zurich
        'Five and a Half Years of Screenprints',
        Flowers Graphics, Flowers East,
        London
        'Fear of God', Riverside Studios,
        London
1995    'Works on Paper', Flowers East at
        London Fields, London
        'Graham Greene and the Jungle of
        Human Dilemma', Flowers East at
        London Fields, London

## Selected Group Exhibitions

1983–84,  'Whitechapel Open', Whitechapel Art
1987     Gallery, London
1983     'Tolly Cobbold', Fitzwilliam Museum,
         Cambridge and nationwide tour
         'Art for Schools', Wells Centre,
         Norfolk
1983–84  Leicestershire Exhibition for Schools
         TWSA National Touring Exhibition
1984–89  Contemporary Art Society Market, 5
         Dials Gallery, London
1985     'Images of War', Chapter Arts Centre,
         Cardiff
1986     'Artists Against Apartheid', Royal
         Festival Hall, London
         'Sixteen', Angela Flowers Gallery,
         London
         'Anti-Thesis', Angela Flowers Gallery,
         London
         Royal Overseas League, London
         'Critic's Space', selected by Fenella
         Crichton, Air Gallery, London

'Small is Beautiful: Part 4', Angela Flowers Gallery, London

1987 'Southbank Picture Show' (prizewinner), Royal Festival Hall, London

'Athena Art Awards', Barbican Art Gallery, London

'Art After Hours', Limelight Club, London

'Self-Portrait', Artsite Gallery, Bath

'Process and Product', Turnpike Gallery, Leigh, Greater Manchester

'Critical Realism', Castle Museum, Nottingham, touring exhibition

'State of the Nation', Herbert Art Gallery, Coventry

'Heroes', Air Gallery, London

'Art for the City', Lloyds Building, London

'Which Side of the Fence?', Imperial War Museum, London

'Small is Beautiful: Part 5', Angela Flowers Gallery, London

'The Big Fight', Vanessa Devereux Gallery, London

'The Other Landscape', Southampton City Art Gallery, Southampton

1988 'New British Painting', Contemporary Arts Centre, Cincinnati, Ohio, touring exhibition

'The Print Show', Angela Flowers Gallery, London

'Contemporary Portraits', Flowers East, London

Royal Overseas League, London

'Wall to Wall Print Show', Pomeroy Purdy Gallery, London

'Nutidskunst', Silkesborg Kunstmuseum, Copenhagen

1989 'Big Paintings', Flowers East, London

'Falklands Factor', Manchester City Art Gallery and touring exhibition

Leicestershire Schools Exhibition

'Confrontation – Three British Artists', Joy Emery Gallery, Michigan, USA

'Fourth International Young Artists Competition', Union of Fine Artists, Sofia, Bulgaria

'The Thatcher Years: An Artistic Retrospective', Flowers East, London

'Portfolio Two', Curwen Gallery, London

1990 'Flowers at Moos', Gallery Moos, New York

'Real Life Stories', Spacex Gallery, Exeter

'Where There is Discord', Cleveland Gallery, Middlesborough

'Angela Flowers Gallery 1990', Barbican Concourse Gallery, London

1991 'Angela Flowers Gallery 1991', Flowers East, London

'Inaugural Exhibition', Lannon Cole Gallery, Chicago

1992 'Artist's Choice', Flowers East, London

1993 'But Big is Better', Flowers East, London

'John Moores 18', Walker Art Gallery, Liverpool

'New Figurative Painting', Salander-O'Reilly Galleries Inc Fred Hoffman, Los Angeles

'Small is Beautiful: Part 9', Flowers East

1993–95 Royal Academy Summer Exhibition, London

1994 'Reflections of Conflict by 16 British and Irish Artists', Wolverhampton Art Gallery and Museums

'An American Passion', McLellan Galleries, Glasgow

1995 'Twenty-Fifth Anniversary Exhibition' Flowers East at London Fields, London

## Residencies and Commissions

1985–86 Artist in Residence, Whitefield School, London

1987 Commissioned poster for London International Mime Festival

1988 Commissioned screenprint for Greenpeace

1990–91 Commissioned exhibition about Ollerton Mining Community, by Nottinghamshire County Council

1991 Official British War Artist, Gulf Crisis

1992 Commissioned cover for *City Limits*

1993 Set design for Salsa Celestina, Palace Theatre, Watford

*The Lives Behind the Lies*, commissioned poster for Amnesty International

1994    Commissioned cover for *The Big Issue*
1995    Commissioned poster for Channel Four
        Sitcom Festival

## Public Collections

Aberdeen Art Gallery
Arthur Anderson & Co.
Arts and Museum Section of Cleveland County
    Library and Leisure Department
British Coal
Chase Manhattan Bank, NA
Christie's Corporate Collection
Contemporary Art Society
Detroit Institute of Fine Art, USA
*The Economist*

*The Financial Times*
Glasgow Museums: Art Gallery and Museum,
    Kelvingrove
Harris Museum and Art Gallery, Preston
Hill Samuel Investment Services Group
Hull City Museums, Art Galleries and Archives
Isle of Man Arts Council
Leicestershire County Council
London Borough of Hammersmith and Fulham
National Power
Paintings in Hospitals
Rugby Museum
Trustees of the Imperial War Museum, London
Unilever
University College of Wales, Aberystwyth
Wolverhampton Museum and Art Gallery

# SELECT BIBLIOGRAPHY

Kent, Sarah, *Time Out*, 12–18 July 1984

*Observer Colour Supplement*, July 1984

Pollitt, Nigel, *City Limits*, 20–26 July 1984

Chapter Arts Centre, Cardiff, catalogue, 1985

Pollitt, Nigel, *City Limits*, 21 December 1985

Kent, Sarah, *Time Out*, 28 March–3 April 1985

Pollitt, Nigel, *City Limits*, 29 March–4 April 1984

Crichton, Fenella, *Critic's Space Catalogue*, Air Gallery, February 1986

Spurling, John, *New Statesman*, 14 February 1986

Kent, Sarah, *Time Out*, 16 February 1986

Spurling, John; *New Statesman*, 9 May 1986

Imperial War Museum catalogue, '*Which Side of the Fence?*', January 1987

Currah, Mark, *City Limits*, 15–22 January 1987

*Time Out*, 4–11 February 1987

*The Other Landscape* catalogue, Southampton City Art Gallery

Kelly, Sean, and Lucie-Smith, Edward, *The Self Portrait – A Modern View* (Sarema Press), 1987

Taylor, Brandon, *Critical Realism* exhibition catalogue, 1987

Lee, David, 'Critical Realism', *Art Review*, August 1987

Hughes, Andrew, *Art Review*, August 1987

Kent, Sarah, *Time Out*, October 1987

Checkland, Sarah, *The Times*, 29 October 1987

Lucie-Smith, Edward, *Bee-keeping in the War-Zone* exhibition catalogue, Angela Flowers Gallery, 1988

Leighton, Nigel, *Against the Wall* exhibition catalogue, Turnpike Gallery, Leigh, 1988

Lucie-Smith, Edward, Cohen, Carolyn, and Higgins, Judith, *New British Painting* (Phaidon Press), 1988

*The Face*, March 1988

Hilton, Tim, *The Guardian*, 2 March 1988

Lee, David, *Art Review*, 11 March 1988

Vaizey, Marina, *Sunday Times*, 13 March 1988

Currah, Mark, *City Limits*, 17 March 1988

Kent, Sarah, *Time Out*, 24–31 August 1988

'Forty Under Forty', *Art and Design Magazine*, 1989

*Company*, February 1989

Currah, Mark, *City Limits*, 20–27 July 1989

Currah, Mark, *City Limits*, 3–10 August 1989

Sebestyen, Amanda, 'Keep the beer-mat flying', *New Statesman*, 4 August 1989

Beckett, Alison, 'Blue Period', *Punch*, 11 August 1989

*Vogue*, August 1989

Jenkins, Peter, *Modern Painters*, Autumn 1989

Bennett, Oliver, 'Canvassing for new buyers', *Sunday Express Magazine*, 29 October 1989

Higgins, Judith, *Sunday Times Magazine*, 11 February 1990

Russell, John, 'The New British Painting', *New York Times*, 9 March 1990

Lee, David, 'Confronting the present', *The Times*, 26 March 1990

Currah, Mark, *City Limits*, 5–12 April 1990

'Peering behind the Northern blind', *London Irish News*, 13 April 1990

Tait, Simon, 'Keane gets contract to paint conflict', *The Times*, 24 August 1990

Barker, Dennis, 'Keane to present his own viewpoint', *The Guardian*, 24 August 1990

'Keane to keep his cool', *Daily Telegraph*, 24 August 1990

'Painter on the frontline', *Today*, 24 August 1990

*The Scotsman*, 24 August 1990

Hunt, Robin, 'The Art of War', *The Sunday Correspondent*, 26 August 1990

Bredin, Lucinda, 'A fighting chance', *Evening Standard*, 30 August 1990

'War artist stands at easel', *The Times*, 5 October 1990

'Artist's View of War: Britain commissions Persian Gulf Crisis Paintings', *The Journal of Art*, Volume 4, No. 2

Bellamy, Christopher, 'Official recorder of Gulf build-up poised for action', *The Independent*, 29 November 1990

'A brush with the military', *The Times*, 5 December 1990

De Jongh, Nicholas, 'Artist after a piece of the action', *The Guardian*, 6 December 1990

Burdick, Larry, 'Style-Makers', *New York Times*, 23 December 1990

'Artist heads for the Gulf', *Evening Standard*, 16 January 1991

'Out of the frame', *The Times*, 18 January 1991

Mackie, Jeannie, 'The art of waging war', *The Guardian*, 18 January 1991

'War artist's trip to Gulf secured', *The Guardian*, 19 January 1991

Greig, Geordie, 'Battling to keep in the picture', *Sunday Times*, 20 January 1991

'Arts of war', *The Times*, 23 January 1991

Porter, Henry, 'Anything but a watercolour war', *Independent on Sunday*, January 1991

Lee, David, *Arts Review*, February 1991

Gayford, Martin, 'Into battle with an easel and paintbrush', *Weekend Telegraph*, 2 February 1991

'Gas masks and sun lotion in a holiday village', *The Guardian*, 6 February 1991

'An artist in the wars', *The Guardian*, 14 February 1991

*Daily Telegraph*, 14 February 1991

*Daily Telegraph*, 23 February 1991

*Daily Telegraph*, 26 February 1991

*The Times*, 22 March 1991

'Brushed Aside', *Daily Telegraph*, 23 March 1991

Hall, Charles, 'Joining the battle home and away', *The Guardian*, 8 April 1991

'Still-Life with Brush', *The Times*, 9 April 1991

*The Guardian*, 12 April 1991

'Keane set for a killing', *The Times*, 17 April 1991

Vaizey, Marina, 'In the coal light of reality', *Sunday Times*, 28 April 1991

Hunt, Robin, 'Brushes with death', *Harpers and Queen*, May 1991

*British Contemporary Art 1910–1990* (Herbert Press), 1991

Schuller, Konrad, 'Peering into the abyss', *The European*, 6–8 September 1991

Fowler, John, 'Portrait of the artist at war', *Glasgow Herald*, 11 october 1991

Hall, Charles, *Art Review*, November 1991

Murphy, Nicola, *The Times*, 6 December 1991

Daneff, Tiffany, and Stringer, Robin, 'Mickey Mouse on the road to hell', *Evening Standard*, 13 January 1992

Thurlbeck, Neville, 'War is . . . Mickey Mouse on a toilet, *Today*, 14 January 1992

Cork, Richard, *The Times*, 15 January 1992

'War artist denies taking Mickey out of Gulf troops', *The Guardian*, 15 January 1992

Cork, Richard, 'Artist defends Mickey Mouse in the Gulf', *The Times*, 15 January 1992

Gillie, Oliver, 'Gulf artist defends scene of war', *The Independent*, 15 January 1992

Deedes, W.F., 'Mickey-taking? I see the filthiness of war', *The Telegraph*, 16 January 1992

'Mickey's War', *The Economist*, 25 January 1992

Foote, Jennifer, 'War and the British Artist', *Newsweek*, 3 February 1992

'Going over the top with Mickey Mouse', *The Guardian*, 13 February 1992

Gillie, Oliver, *The Independent*, 15 March 1992

*The Sun*, 15 January 1992

Whittle, Lisa, 'Alien Landscapes', *New Statesman and Society*, 20 March 1992

*The Journal*, 25 March 1992

Brown, Andrew, 'Gulf painting withdrawn by war museum', *The Independent*, 27 March 1992

Bussmann, Tom, 'Gallery that's tiptoeing over the top', *The Guardian*, 28 March 1992

'Mickey Mouse's Gulf War', *Amateur Photographer*, 28 March 1992

Loppert, Susan, 'Mickey Mouse and the Great Dictator', *Galleries*, April 1992

Dorment, Richard, 'Losing the war with a brush and palette', *Daily Telegraph*, 1 April 1992

Hilton, Tim, 'Putting on the war paint', *The Guardian*, 2 April 1992

*City Limits*, 2–9 April 1992

Russell Taylor, John, *The Times*, 3 April 1992

*The Guardian*, 4 April 1992

Lubbock, Tom, *The Independent*, 5 April 1992

Whitford, Frank, 'Scenes from a theatre of war', *Sunday Times*, 5 April 1992

Feaver, William, 'Mickey gets in a mess of war', *The Observer*, 5 April 1992

McEwen, John, *Sunday Telegraph*, 5 April 1992

Kent, Sarah, 'A brush with war', *Time Out*, 8–15 April 1992

Sewell, Brian, 'Caught in the crossfire', *Evening Standard*, 9 April 1992

*The Guardian*, 11 April 1992

Packer, William, 'Gulf War Paintings', *Financial Times*, 14 April 1992

Knight, Karl, *The Times*, 14 April 1992

Kent, Sarah, *Time Out*, 15 April 1992

Foots, Jennifer, 'War and the British Artist: Does *Mickey Mouse at the Front* say it all?', *Newsweek*, 15 April 1992

*The Guardian*, 18 April 1992

*The Independent*, 21 April 1992

Artner, Alan G., 'Keane visions focus on war, urban poor', *Chicago Tribune*, 24 April 1992

Lee, David, 'Profile', *Art Review*, May 1992

Buck, Louisa, *Vogue*, May 1992

*Socialist*, May 1992

Buck, Louisa, 'Brushes with death', *GQ Magazine*, May 1992

*The Independent*, 5 May 1992

The Times, 9 May 1992

Hilton, Tim, *The Guardian*, 9 May 1992

Henry, Clare, 'Images of gloom', *The Herald*, 15 May 1992

Britten, Bob, 'Art of war in the Gulf', *New Times*, 16 May 1992

*The Independent on Sunday*, 24 May 1992

*The Art Quarterly*, No. 10, Summer 1992

Sadler, Rosalin, 'Apocalypse all ways', *Modern Painters*, Summer 1992

'Dal nostro pittoro sul fronte dei massacri', *Avvenimenti*, 30 September 1992

Woods, Alan, 'Gulf War realities', *The Herald*, 24 November 1992

Davies, Russell, 'Cry Coal', *Telegraph Weekend Magazine*, 30 January 1993

*Daily Telegraph*, 3 July 1993

Kent, Sarah, 'Keen and fable', *Time Out*, 14–21 July 1993

*Independent on Sunday*, 1 August 1993

Russell-Taylor, John, *The Times*, 13 August 1993

'Artist as Witness', *Central America Report*, Autumn 1992

*The London Magazine*, October 1993

Gale, Iain, 'War on the home front', *The Independent*, 9 November 1993

Lester, Anthony, 'The Art of War', *The Big Issue*, 9–15 November 1993

Delaney, Greg, 'Buddies', *Arena*, March 1994

Howe, Darcus, 'The new Union Jack', *The Big Issue*, 17–23 October 1994

Gough, Paul, 'The Tyranny of Seeing', *Art Review*, November 1994

Baddeley, Oriana, 'British Art – Defining the 90s', *Art and Design*, May 1995

## Selected TV

*Review Special*, BBC2, 9 March 1988

*01 for London*, ITV, March 1988

*BBC Breakfast Time*, 23 August 1990

*Frank Bough interview*, Sky TV, 30 August 1990

*The VIP Show*, BSkyB, 5 October 1990

*Box Office*, Channel Four, 26 November 1990

*The Late Show*, BBC2, 23 January 1991

*Sky News*, February 1991

*The Late Show*, BBC2, 12 March 1991

*ZDF*, August 1991

*The Late Show*, BBC2, 20 January 1992

*Thames News*, ITV, 24 March 1992

*ZDF*, March 1992

*Live and Direct*, Granada, 25 November 1994

## Selected Radio

*Big City*, Radio London, 5 March 1988

*Midweek*, BBC Radio 4, 19 September 1990

*Outlook*, BBC World Service, 9 April 1991

*Kaleidoscope*, BBC Radio 4, 14 April 1991

*Tuesday Lives*, BBC Radio 4, 12 November 1991

*Kaleidoscope*, BBC Radio 4, 2 December 1991

*The World Today*, BBC World Service, February 1992

*Diana Luke Show*, GLR, March 1992

*Outlook*, BBC World Service, 27 May 1992

*Omnibus*, BBC World Service, November 1992

*Night Waves*, BBC Radio 4, 7 July 1993

*Kaleidoscope*, BBC Radio 4, 30 September 1994

*Peter Curran Show*, GLR, November 1994

*From Our Own Correspondent*, BBC Radio 4, 25 February 1995

GCCC Library
101 College Drive
Hot Springs, AR 71913